美国
文化与口语

第二版

蒋景阳　周颂波 ◎主编

American Culture
and
Oral English

（2nd Edition）

ZHEJIANG UNIVERSITY PRESS
浙江大学出版社
·杭州·

图书在版编目（CIP）数据

美国文化与口语 ： 英文 ／ 蒋景阳，周颂波主编. --
2版. -- 杭州 ： 浙江大学出版社，2023.8
　　ISBN 978-7-308-23875-5

　　Ⅰ．①美… Ⅱ．①蒋… ②周… Ⅲ．①英语－口语－
高等学校－教材②美国－概况 Ⅳ．①H319.9②K971.2

　　中国国家版本馆CIP数据核字(2023)第099356号

美国文化与口语（第二版）

MEIGUO WENHUA YU KOUYU（DI-ER BAN）

蒋景阳　周颂波　主编

策　　划	李　晨
责任编辑	郑成业
责任校对	陈丽勋
封面设计	闰江文化
出版发行	浙江大学出版社
	（杭州市天目山路148号　　邮政编码　310007）
	（网址：http://www.zjupress.com）
排　　版	杭州林智广告有限公司
印　　刷	杭州捷派印务有限公司
开　　本	787mm×1092mm　1/16
印　　张	10
字　　数	323千
版 印 次	2023年8月第2版　2023年8月第1次印刷
书　　号	ISBN 978-7-308-23875-5
定　　价	35.00元

浙江大学出版社市场运营中心联系方式：0571-88925591；http://zjdxcbs.tmall.com

前　言
Preface

　　习近平总书记在党的二十大报告中指出，"构建人类命运共同体是世界各国人民前途所在"，并呼吁世界各国"尊重世界文明多样性，以文明交流超越文明隔阂、文明互鉴超越文明冲突、文明共存超越文明优越，共同应对各种全球性挑战"。

　　《美国文化与口语》（第二版）将国家和社会的发展需要作为教材编写的出发点和立足点。它的出版不仅响应了国家和时代对于文化交流的迫切需求，同时又能很大程度地满足学生对知识与能力的渴望。

　　众所周知，语言与文化是密不可分的。语言是文化的组成部分和重要载体，而文化是语言的土壤。对于英语学习者而言，熟悉英语国家的社会与文化，能使谈话更加深入、得体，使交流更加顺畅、有效。目前的英语教材，基本上只注重学生语言能力的提高，而文化方面的教材，又大多局限于文化的灌输，能够有机地把文化知识与语言能力，尤其是口语能力结合起来的教材，寥寥无几。本教材的编写旨在弥补这方面的不足，将文化与口语结合起来，使学生在了解熟悉美国文化的同时，提高口语交际能力。

　　在教材内容上，我们力求提供真实的语言素材以及符合现实生活的口语活动。本教材共分16章，题材内容包罗万象，涵盖了美国社会和文化的各个领域：美国地理、历史、教育、大众媒体、经济、工作与公司文化、运动、休闲娱乐、音乐、社会问题、肢体语言、交通、购物、饮食文化、动物保护、公共场合的行为等。每章除了介绍美国文化的阅读材料，还提供了切合主题且生动有趣的视听内容，以及模拟真实语言使用场景的丰富多样的口语实践活动，从而使学生能够将所获得的文化知识和语汇有机地结合到口语活动中，既领会了文化知识，又锻炼了口语能力。相信学生在使用本教材后，不但能够通过读、视、听、说等语言活动，深入了解美国社会与文化的方方面面，而且能够切实提高自己的口语交流能力。

本教材"视"和"听"的内容丰富多样，多渠道展现了美国的社会和文化，并且配有二维码，只需用手机轻轻一扫就能看到或听到对应的视听内容。此外，在第一版的基础上，我们对部分内容和活动进行了更新和改编，新增的活动和资源充分体现了课程思政的理念，引导学生进行中美文化的交流互鉴，致力于建设一个开放包容的世界。同时，培养学生的跨文化意识和跨文化交际能力，帮助学生树立文化自信。

本教材的编写者为：蒋景阳、周颂波、熊海虹、方富民、王小潞、闻人行和傅莹。所有编写者都有在美国授课或游学的经历，因此所编写的内容和设计的活动贴近现实生活，体现了时代特征。美国专家Maxine Huffman和Don Huffman也为教材的编写提供了大量的材料，并担任了主审。此外，还要感谢方竹静、柏卉、邓望学、易兰和陈晶晶，他们对口语活动的样本提供了帮助。

本书可以用作英语专业低年级本科生或非英语专业本科生的必修课、选修课或通识课教材，也适用于希望了解美国文化且有一定英语基础的读者。

编　者
2023年7月

CONTENTS

Chapter 1

Geography

Part A   Preview

A Quiz on the American Geography

Directions: *Work in pairs and do the following quiz on the American geography.*

1. What is the total area of the US including Alaska and Hawaii? _____
   A. Over 9 million square kilometers.
   B. Between 8 million and 9 million square kilometers.
   C. Between 7 million and 8 million square kilometers.

2. What is the distance from west to east of the continental US? _____
   A. 5,500 km.   B. 5,000 km.   C. 4,500 km.

3. What are the two youngest states of the US? _____
   A. Louisiana and Virginia.   B. Texas and Florida.   C. Alaska and Hawaii.

4. Match the state with the country from whom it was bought.

Alaska	Spain
Louisiana	Russia
Florida	France

5. Where are they situated?

(1)   (2)    (3)

(4)    (5)    (6)

Write down in the blanks the cities in which the above landmarks are situated.

(1) _____ (2) _____ (3) _____

(4) _____ (5) _____ (6) _____

6. Where is the US farm belt located? _____

　　A. Northeast.　　　　B. West.　　　　C. Midwest.　　　　D. Southeast.

7. In which city of Florida is Disney World located? _____

　　A. Orlando.　　　　B. Tampa.　　　　C. Miami.　　　　D. Fort Lauderdale.

8. Which of the following is the "City of Skyscrapers"? _____

　　A. Los Angeles.　　　B. Chicago.　　　C. New York.　　　D. San Francisco.

9. On which mountain are the faces of four US presidents carved? _____

　　A. Mount Vernon.　　B. Mount McKinley.　C. Mount Pleasant.　D. Mount Rushmore.

10. Which is the largest state in the US in terms of land area? _____

　　A. Texas.　　　　B. Alaska.　　　　C. California.　　　　D. Montana.

11. Which river forms a natural border between the US and Mexico? _____

　　A. Red River.　　　B. Mississippi River.　C. Rio Grande.　　D. Gila River.

12. Las Vegas (拉斯维加斯) is located in _____.

　　A. California　　　　B. Nevada　　　　C. Arizona

13. San Diego (圣地亚哥) borders _____.

　　A. Canada　　　　B. Mexico　　　　C. the Atlantic

14. Kansas City is in both Kansas and which other state of the US? _____

　　A. Missouri.　　　　B. Nebraska.　　　　C. Oklahoma.

15. Write the full names of the abbreviated state names.

　　ND _____　　MN _____　　WI _____

　　OK _____　　AR _____　　LA _____

　　GA _____　　CO _____　　WM _____

Part B　Viewing

Scan and Watch

The Western Valleys and the Columbia Plateau

Vocabulary in the Viewing

Imperial Valley 因皮里尔谷　　　　Coastal Ranges 海岸山脉

Sierra Nevada 内华达山脉　　　　orchard 果园

vineyard 葡萄园　　　　Willamette Valley 威拉米特谷

Oregon Trail 俄勒冈小道　　　　the Cascades 喀斯喀特山脉

hydroelectric power 水电	Portland 波特兰
spectacular 壮观的	Columbia River Gorge 哥伦比亚河谷
towering waterfall 高耸的瀑布	plateau 平原

Directions: *Watch the video about the Western Valleys and the Columbia Plateau and fill in the missing information.*

The Pacific region is home to large and productive 1. _____. The Central Valley has long 2. _____, moderate 3. _____, and 4. _____. Among many other agricultural products, this area has lots of 5. _____ orchards, 6. _____ orchards, 7. _____, and many types of 8. _____.

Willamette Valley of Oregon produces 9. _____ of crops because it has a 10. _____, 11. _____ piece of land with 12. _____ climate, and 13. _____. The water of the Columbia River is used for 14. _____ and to generate 15. _____.

The Columbia Plateau is very productive, but has 16. _____ climate and almost 17. _____. So the main agricultural products grown there are the 18. _____ and 19. _____.

Part C Reading for Information

Physical Environment in the US

Geographical Divisions

①The dominant geographical features of the United States tend to extend north-south across the country. The interior of the country is a vast lowland that stretches from the Gulf of Mexico to the Canadian border and then on to Alaska. Geographers place this expanse of flat land and gently **rolling**[1] hills in three different **physiographic**[2] regions—the Atlantic and Gulf coastal plains, the interior lowland, and the Canadian Shield.

②The Atlantic and Gulf coastal plains reach north along the east coast of the United States as far as the southern margins of **New England**[3]. Underlying this area are beds of young, soft, easily eroded rock **deposited**[4] in recent geologic time as shallow seas. These low plains extend well out under the ocean surface to form a **continental shelf**[5], which in places extends as much as 400 kilometers beyond the shore.

③The interior lowland, although noticeably hillier than the coastal plains, has almost no rough **terrain**[6]. This region is like a saucer, turned up at the edges and covered with **sedimentary**[7] rocks.

④The character of this massive interior lowland area has had a number of important influences on the economic and settlement history of the United States. In addition to the vast agricultural potential it provides, half the country can be crossed without encountering significant **topographic**[8] barriers. This facilitated the integration of both this region and the distant West into the economic fabric of the country. Nearly all of the interior lowland is drained by the Mississippi River or its **tributaries**[9]. This assisted regional integration by providing a transport and economic focus for the land west of **the Appalachian Mountains**[10].

⑤North and northeast of the central lowland is the Canadian Shield, where old, hard **crystalline rocks**[11] lie at the surface. Farther south in the lowlands, similar rocks are covered by the sedimentary beds deposited under the sea that once filled the midsection of the country. Erosion has worn down the surface of the Shield into a lowland of small local **relief**[12].

Climate

⑥The United States is mainly situated in the northern **temperate zone**[13]. But, owing to its large size and varied landforms, it has different types of climate in different areas.

⑦The climate of New England is relatively cold. The winters are long and hard. In many parts of Maine, there is snow on the ground from early November to late May. The summers are short and warm. The fall, however, is a beautiful time of year. In the fall, the leaves of trees turn different colors, giving the hills and woods a bright look.

⑧The climate of the Middle Atlantic States region is generally pleasant. There are four definite seasons. The winters are cold and snowy, and the springs are warm, with plenty of rain to help the growth of crops. Summers are short and hot but pleasant, while the falls are cool.

⑨The South enjoys a warm climate and abundant rainfall. The climate, however, varies with the geographical position of each state. Virginia and North Carolina have a temperate climate like that of Maryland. In southern Florida, on the other hand, the climate is almost tropical. Some states in this region are sometimes **harassed**[14] by the disaster of **hurricanes**[15].

⑩Since **the Great Plains**[16] stretch from the Canadian border to Texas, the climate in this region varies widely. North Dakota has extreme temperatures, strong winds, and low **precipitation**[17]. Oklahoma, on the other hand, has a more temperate climate. The open treeless, unbroken land offers little protection against storms or against the rapid changes of weather that occur in this area. In many parts of the plains states there is little rain. Extended periods of very hot weather during a summer without rain may not only destroy crops but also turn the land into dust.

⑪The climate of the Midwest is temperate. The region lies in a great valley between **the Allegheny Mountains**[18] to the east and the Great Plains and **Rocky Mountains**[19] to the west. This is a largely open country, and the wind blows freely, often bringing sudden and extreme changes in temperature. Midwest summers are sometimes very hot; winters are sometimes extremely cold.

⑫The states west of the Rocky Mountains have sharply different climatic conditions. This is largely because of the effects of the mountain ranges and the Pacific Ocean. Winds from the

Pacific bring plenty of rain, yet these winds are conditioned by the mountains along the coast. Generally speaking, the western slopes of the Coastal Mountains are cool, rainy, and cloudy. The part of Washington near the Pacific Ocean has the highest rainfall in the country. But after crossing these mountains, very little rain falls and deserts appear.

Vegetation

⑬The "natural" vegetation, if it ever existed, has been so substantially removed, rearranged, and replaced that it seldom is found now. In the Southeast, for example, the original mixed **broadleaf and needleleaf forests**[20] were cut and replaced by the economically more important needleleaf forests. The grasses of the plains and prairies are mostly European imports. Most of what **climax vegetation**[21] remains is in the West and North.

⑭There are several ways of dividing vegetation regions. Perhaps the simplest is to divide the United States into three broad categories—forest, grasslands, and **scrublands**[22]. Forests once covered most of the East, the central and northern Pacific Coast, the higher **elevations**[23] of the West, and a broad band across the interior North.

⑮Grasslands cover much of the interior lowlands, including nearly all of the Great Plains from Texas and New Mexico to the Canadian border. This is an area of generally **sub-humid climate**[24] where precipitation amounts are not adequate to support tree growth.

⑯Scrublands usually develop under dry conditions. They are concentrated in the lowlands of the interior West. Actual vegetation varies from the **cacti**[25] of the Southwest to the dense, brushy **chaparral**[26] of southern California and the **mesquite**[27] of Texas.

Natural Resources

⑰The United States is a land rich in natural resources. Some of these resources, such as water, iron **ore**[28], coal, oil, silver, and gold, are especially plentiful in the country.

⑱America has a large deposit of iron ore. The nation produces more than 80 million tons of iron a year. For many years, iron ore came primarily from the Great Lake region of Minnesota and Michigan, but the mines were severely **depleted**[29] during the two World Wars. The richer ores are exhausted, though large amounts of lower-grade materials remain and form the basis of a thriving industry. Iron ores are also mined in Missouri, New York, Utah and Wyoming.

⑲Coal is another major natural resource found in large quantities in the US which can last for hundreds of years. Coal deposits are widely distributed in the country. Most of coal reserves are to be found in the Appalachians, the Central Plain, and the Rockies.

⑳America, very rich in oil, was once the largest oil producing country in the world. Oil wells in the United States produce more than 3,200 million barrels of petroleum a year. The production, processing and marketing of such petroleum products as gasoline and oil make up one of America's largest industries. Most domestic production of oil and natural gas comes from **offshore**[30] areas of Louisiana and Texas, and from **onshore**[31] areas of Texas, Oklahoma, and California. Although the oil production in the US is very large, her big consumption has made America insufficient in oil supply. The shortage of domestic supplies of energy was forcefully publicized by the Arab oil **embargo**[32] of 1973–1974. Until this embargo most Americans did not realize that the United States does not have enough energy to meet its ever-growing needs.

㉑America enjoys abundant water resources. Today the rivers and streams of America furnish 63 % of the water supply for cities, towns and farmlands, 93% of the water used by industry, and almost all of the water used to create electric power. Unlike some other countries, America as a whole has little trouble as caused by the shortage of fresh water.

㉒America has also plenty of fertile soil. Farmlands in the United States make up about 12% of the **arable**[33] lands in the world, and they are among the richest and most productive. Of the 2.3 billion acres of land in the 50 states an estimated 300 million acres are planted annually. The country's very large **acreage**[34] of highly productive farmlands could be expected to continue to supply the nation generously, with substantial surplus for export.

Additional Material

(1,403 words)

Notes to the Passage

1. rolling 起伏的
2. physiographic 地形学的
3. New England 新英格兰地区
4. deposit 沉积
5. continental shelf 大陆架
6. terrain 地形
7. sedimentary 沉积性的
8. topographic 地形（学）的
9. tributary 支流
10. the Appalachian Mountains 阿巴拉契亚山脉
11. crystalline rock 结晶岩
12. relief（地势的）起伏
13. temperate zone 温带
14. harass 袭扰
15. hurricane 飓风
16. the Great Plains（密西西比河流域以西的）大平原
17. precipitation 降水量
18. the Allegheny Mountains 阿勒格尼山脉（从宾夕法尼亚州中北向西南延伸至弗吉尼亚州西南部，绵亘800多千米）
19. Rocky Mountains 落基山脉
20. broadleaf and needleleaf forests 阔叶和针叶林
21. climax vegetation 顶级植被
22. scrubland 灌木丛林地
23. elevation 高地
24. sub-humid climate 半湿润气候
25. cacti（单数cactus）仙人掌
26. chaparral 茂密的树丛
27. mesquite 豆科灌木
28. ore 矿
29. deplete 耗尽
30. offshore 近海的

31. onshore 陆地上的

32. embargo 禁运

33. arable 适于耕种的

34. acreage 英亩数

Reading Exercise

Directions: *After you read the passage, answer the following questions or complete the sentences with the information you get from the passage.*

1. Which of the following has vast flat land and gently rolling hills? _____
   A. The Atlantic and Gulf coastal plains.
   B. The interior lowland.
   C. The Canadian Shield.
   D. All the above.

2. The landform of the interior lowland area assisted all of the following EXCEPT _____.
   A. agricultural gains
   B. the integration of national economy
   C. easy transportation
   D. the formation of sedimentary rocks

3. Compared with the rock deposit of the Atlantic and Gulf coastal plains, the rocks in the Canadian Shield are _____.
   A. older and harder
   B. younger and softer
   C. more easily eroded
   D. lower and flatter

4. In the United States, the climate _____.
   A. is mild and pleasant throughout the year
   B. is humid and rainy in the Great Basin of the Southwest
   C. varies widely due to its immense size and spread of topology
   D. is mild and sunny in spring and fall and wet and cold in winter

5. Which area has the most pleasant climate? _____
   A. The Midwest states.
   B. The Middle Atlantic states.
   C. The Great Plains states.
   D. Southern Florida.

6. The climate west of the Rocky Mountains is greatly affected by _____.
   A. the mountains and the Pacific
   B. the Great Plains
   C. desert-like dryness
   D. hurricanes and tornadoes

7. Why were the original forests in the Southeast cut down? _____
   A. To rearrange the ecological structure of the area.
   B. To replace the old forests with new ones from Europe.
   C. To grow trees which yield higher economical benefits.
   D. To increase the variety of actual vegetation.

8. What is true of the iron ores in the United States? _____
   A. They are depleted.
   B. Most of them produce iron of low grade.

C. They are no longer mined.

D. They are the basic support of a prosperous country.

9. The natural resources of the US are _____.

 A. limited   B. exhausted   C. evenly distributed D. abundant

10. America does not have enough _____ supply to meet its domestic needs.

 A. water   B. oil supply   C. arable land   D. grain supply

Part D Speaking Activities

1. A Travel Plan

Directions: *A group of Chinese university students are going to visit the US for the first time during their summer vacation. It will be a 14-day tour. They want to visit as many places as they can, but they may have different places in mind. They are now talking with a travel agent about it.*

Work in groups of 4 to 6. One of you is going to act the role of the travel agent, and the rest are the students. Discuss and try to come up with an exciting travel plan for the whole group. You may refer to the Preview exercises and the reading material for places of interest.

2. Immigrants in the US

Directions: *Read the following statistics about immigrants in the US. Then work in groups to discuss the questions that follow.*

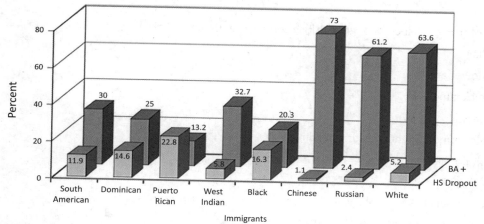

Notes: "BA +" refers to the proportion of respondents who have completed a four-year college degree or have attained a post-graduate education, "HS Dropout" refers to the proportion of respondents who dropped out of high school.

Figure A   Educational Attainment of Second Generation by Group (Aged 25 and Older)

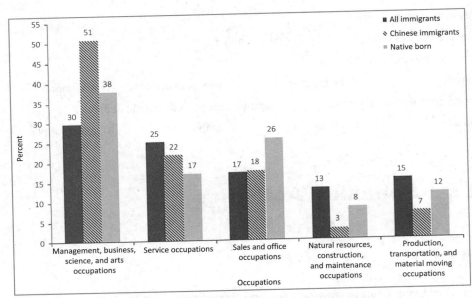

Figure B   Occupation Percentage of Immigrants in the US

(1) How does the educational attainment of Chinese descendants compare with other groups? What may be the reasons for their higher attainment?

(2) What are the differences between the occupations of Chinese immigrants and the immigrants from other countries?

3. Facts about the US States

Directions: *Choose one state of the US and start gathering all the information you need (such as text, pictures, video and sound) to give an A+ class presentation about the state. You may include the following factors:*

- origin of the state (such as original British colony, Spanish colony, etc.)
- state flag
- state flower and tree
- state nickname
- state capital
- landmarks (monuments, historic buildings)
- present population
- major cities
- famous universities and colleges
- kinds of food representative of the state
- crops grown in the state
- historical events
- places of interest

Chapter 2

History

Part A   Preview

A Quiz on the US History

Directions: *Work in pairs and do the following quiz on the US history.*

1. What's the name of the US flag?

_____

2. What are the colors of the stripes and stars on the US flag? _____

   A. White and blue stripes and blue stars in a white field.

   B. Red and white stripes and white stars in a blue field.

   C. Black and white stripes and red stars in a yellow field.

3. What is the national anthem of the United States? _____

   A. *The Star Spangled Banner*.   B. *Land of My Fathers*.   C. *Land That I Love*.

4. What is the Statue of Liberty mostly made of? _____

   A. Bronze.   B. Steel.   C. Copper.

5. What was the source of the following phrase, "Government of the people, by the people, for the people"? _____

   A. The speech "I Have a Dream."   B. The Declaration of Independence.

   C. The US Constitution.   D. The Gettysburg Address.

6. Enter in the boxes the number corresponding to the right answer.

☐ Benjamin Franklin   (1) 42nd President of the United States

☐ Abraham Lincoln   (2) statesman who negotiated Treaty of Paris

☐ Henry Kissinger   (3) 16th President of the United States

☐ Bill Clinton   (4) 56th United States Secretary of State

7. The most famous tragedy in US history was the bombing of Pearl Harbor on December 7, 1941. When did the US declare war on Japan? _____

A. December 7.   B. December 8.

C. December 9.   D. December 10.

8. On May 4th, 1970, National Guard troops opened fire on college students protesting President Nixon's invasion of Cambodia. On what college campus did this shooting take place? _____

A. Kent State University.   B. Colorado University.

C. Jackson State University.   D. South Carolina State University.

9. On April 16th, 2007, on the campus of Virginia Tech University in Blacksburg, Virginia, a student went on a shooting rampage (乱枪扫射) which became the deadliest shooting in US history. Including the perpetrator (行凶者), how many people were killed? _____

A. 41.   B. 38.   C. 33.   D. 27.

10. What does "Philadelphia" mean in Greek? _____

A. Brotherly love.   B. Heavenly Paradise.

C. Courage.   D. Peace.

11. What was the Mayflower Compact?

_____

12. Which of the following was the first college founded in the thirteen colonies? _____

A. Columbia University.   B. Harvard University.

C. Georgetown University.   D. Yale University.

13. Who was the youngest man elected president in the United States? _____

A. John F. Kennedy.   B. Bill Clinton.

C. Barack Hussein Obama.   D. Franklin D. Roosevelt.

14. The US Constitution is the world's _____ constitution.

A. newest   B. oldest   C. longest   D. shortest

15. Who wrote the major part of the Declaration of Independence? _____

A. Thomas Jefferson.   B. George Washington.

C. Benjamin Franklin.   D. Robert R. Livingston.

16. Which president was born on July 4? _____

A. Thomas Jefferson.   B. John Adams.

C. James Monroe.   D. Calvin Coolidge.

17. What did Nathan Hale say on his way to the gallows (绞刑架)? _____

A. "Give me liberty or give me death!"

B. "I only regret that I have but one life to lose for my country."

C. "Long live the United States of America."

D. "He that lives upon hope will die fasting."

18. Who am I?

A. I wrote the famous pamphlet *Common Sense* urging the colonists to make a clean break with England. Who am I? _____.

B. My last name starts with an "A." I dedicated my life to obtain women's rights, including the right to vote. Who am I? _____.

C. My last name starts with a "K." I was a champion for racial equality in the US. Who am I?

_____.

D. My last name starts with an "A." I was the first person to walk on the moon. Who am I?

_____.

E. This word starts with a "P." We are a group of people who sailed to Plymouth Rock in the 1600s and settled in the New World. Who are we? _____.

Part B   Viewing

Scan and Watch

The Statue of Liberty

Vocabulary in the Viewing

West Indies 西印度群岛	skyline 地平线
harbor 港口	forge a bond 结成联盟
brotherhood 兄弟般的关系	sculptor 雕塑家
sculpture 雕像	commemorate 纪念
Bedloe's Island 白德路岛（亦称自由女神岛）	pedestal 底座
legal 法律的	

Directions: *Watch the video about the Statue of Literby and choose the right answer to each question.*

1. What was the original purpose of France in building the Statue of Liberty?

A. To create a reminder of America's ideals of equality and opportunity.

B. To present it to President Grant and other prominent Americans.

C. To greet immigrants who arrived in New York by boat.

D. To commemorate the American Declaration of Independence.

2. What was true of the Americans' early attitude toward the Statue of Liberty?

A. They showed reluctance.

B. They welcomed the idea.

C. The statue was fine, but the pedestal needed change.

D. The statue was fine, but they couldn't find a place to put it.

3. When was the Statue of Liberty dedicated in New York?

A. In October, 1783.　　　　　　　　　B. In June, 1874.

C. In October, 1886.　　　　　　　　　D. In May, 1871.

4. According to the video, what was the percentage of immigrants who were rejected entry at Ellis Island and the Immigration Processing Center in New York harbor?

A. 2%.　　　　　B. 10%.　　　　　C. 50%.　　　　　D. 75%.

5. What was true of the image that the early immigrants had of America before they came here?

A. All the houses were decorated with gold.

B. It was very difficult to become its citizen.

C. New York and the Statue of Liberty were the center of America.

D. It was a land of great wealth.

Part C　Reading for Information

The Road to American Independence

"The Revolution was effected before the war commenced.
The Revolution was in the hearts and minds of the people."

—*Former President John Adams, 1818*

A New Colonial System

①After the French and Indian War, Britain needed a new imperial structure. However, the colonies, long accustomed to independence, were demanding more, not less, freedom.

②Fast increasing in population, and needing more land for settlement, various colonies claimed the right to extend their boundaries as far west as the Mississippi River. The British government, fearing that this would provoke Indian wars, wanted the lands to be opened to colonists more slowly. The **Royal Proclamation**[1] of 1763 reserved all the western territory between the Alleghenies, Florida, the Mississippi River and Quebec for use by Native Americans. This measure, in the eyes of the colonists, constituted a **high-handed**[2] disregard of their right.

③More serious in its impact was the new financial policy of the British government, which needed more money to support its growing empire. The money needed would have to be **extracted**[3] from the colonists in the form of taxes.

④One of the new taxes was the "Stamp Act," which provided that **revenue stamps**[4] be added to all newspapers, pamphlets, licenses, **leases**[5] or other legal documents, the revenue to be used for "defending, protecting and securing" the colonies.

⑤The Stamp Act **bore** equally **on**[6] people who did any kind of business. Thus it aroused the hostility of the most powerful and **articulate**[7] groups in the American population: journalists, lawyers, **clergymen**[8], merchants and businessmen.

⑥The Massachusetts Assembly invited all the colonies to appoint delegates to the so-called Stamp Act Congress in New York, held in October 1765. The congress asserted that "no taxes ever have been or can be **constitutionally**[9] imposed on them, but by their respective **legislatures**[10]," and that the Stamp Act had a "**manifest**[11] tendency to **subvert**[12] the rights and liberties of the colonists."

⑦In 1766 Parliament yielded, **repealing**[13] the Stamp Act; but a year later, new duties on colonial imports of paper, glass, lead and tea exported from Britain to the colonies were introduced.

⑧Merchants resorted to non-importation agreements, and people **made do with**[14] local products. Colonists, for example, dressed in **homespun**[15] clothing and found substitutes for tea. They used homemade paper and their houses went unpainted. In Boston, enforcement of the new regulations provoked violence. Faced with such opposition, Parliament repealed all the duties except that on tea, which was a luxury item in the colonies.

Boston "Tea Party"

⑨In 1773, the British government granted the powerful East India Company a monopoly on all tea exported to the colonies. Aroused by the monopolistic practice involved as well as the loss of the tea trade, colonial traders joined the **radicals**[16] **agitating**[17] for independence.

⑩In ports up and down the Atlantic coast, new shipments of tea were either returned to England or warehoused. On the night of December 16, 1773, a band of men disguised as **Mohawk**

Indians[18] boarded three British ships lying at anchor in Boston and dumped their tea cargo into Boston harbor.

⑪Official opinion in Britain almost **unanimously**[19] condemned the Boston Tea Party as an act of **vandalism**[20] and advocated legal measures to **bring** the **insurgent**[21] colonists **into line**[22].

The Coercive[23] Acts

⑫Parliament responded with what the colonists called the "Coercive or Intolerable Acts." The first act, Boston Port Bill closed the port of Boston until the tea was paid for—an action that threatened the very life of the city, for to prevent Boston from having access to the sea meant economic disaster. Other acts banned most town meetings held without the governor's consent. Instead of isolating Massachusetts as Parliament intended, these acts rallied its sister colonies to its aid.

⑬Colonial representatives met in Philadelphia at a meeting that came to be known as the First Continental Congress on September 5, 1774, "to consult upon the present unhappy state of the Colonies." The division of opinion in the colonies posed a genuine **dilemma**[24] for the delegates. They would have to give an appearance of firm **unanimity**[25] to induce the British government to compromise and, at the same time, they would have to avoid any show of **radicalism**[26] or spirit of independence that would alarm more moderate Americans. A cautious **keynote speech**[27] ended with adoption of a set of resolutions, among them, the right of the colonists to "life, liberty and property," and the right of provincial legislatures to set "all cases of taxation and internal polity."

⑭The most important action taken by the Congress, however, was the formation of a "Continental Association," which provided for the renewal of a trade **boycott**[28]. They began collecting military supplies and **mobilizing**[29] troops.

⑮But George III had no intention of making concessions. In September 1774, scorning a **petition**[30] by **Philadelphia Quakers**[31], he wrote, "**The die is now cast**[32], the Colonies must either submit or triumph."

The Revolution Begins

⑯General Thomas Gage, an Englishman, commanded the troops at Boston. When news reached him that the Massachusetts colonists were collecting powder and military stores at the town of Concord, 32 kilometers away, Gage sent his soldiers to **confiscate**[33] these **munitions**[34].

⑰After a night of marching, the British troops reached the village of Lexington on April 19, 1775, and saw a grim band of 70 Minutemen—so named because they were said to be ready to fight in a minute—through the early morning mist. The Minutemen intended only a silent protest, but Major John Pitcairn, the leader of the British troops, yelled, "**Disperse**[35], you damned rebels! You dogs, run!" The Americans were withdrawing when someone fired a shot, which led the British troops to fire at the Minutemen, leaving 8 dead and 10 wounded. It was, in the often quoted phrase of Ralph Waldo Emerson, "the shot heard round the world."

⑱The British pushed on to Concord. In the meantime, American forces in the countryside mobilized, moved toward Concord and inflicted **casualties**[36] on the British, who began the long return to Boston. All along the road, however, behind stone walls and houses, **militiamen**[37] from "every **Middlesex**[38] village and farm" made targets of the bright red coats of the British soldiers. By the time the weary soldiers stumbled into Boston, they suffered more than 250 killed and wounded. The Americans lost 93 men.

⑲While the alarms of Lexington and Concord were still **resounding**[39], the Second Continental Congress met in Philadelphia on May 10, 1775. The Congress voted to go to war, appointing Colonel George Washington as commander-in-chief of the American forces. King George III issued a proclamation on August 23, 1775, declaring the colonies to be in a state of rebellion.

Common Sense and Independence

⑳In January 1776, Thomas Paine, a political theorist and writer who had come to America from England in 1774, published a 50-page pamphlet, *Common Sense*. Within three months, 100,000 copies of the pamphlet were sold. Paine attacked the idea of **hereditary monarchy**[40], declaring that one honest man was worth more to society than "all the **crowned**[41] **ruffians**[42] that ever lived." He presented the alternatives—either continued submission to a **tyrannical**[43] king and an **outworn**[44] government, or liberty and happiness as a self-sufficient, independent republic. Circulated throughout the colonies, *Common Sense* helped to crystallize the desire for separation.

㉑Largely Jefferson's work, the Declaration of Independence, adopted July 4, 1776, not only announced the birth of a new nation, but also set forth a philosophy of human freedom:

㉒"We hold these truths to be self-evident, that all men are created equal, that they are endowed by their Creator with certain unalienable Rights, that among these are Life, Liberty and the pursuit of Happiness."

㉓To fight for American independence was to fight for a government based on popular consent in place of a government by a king who had "combined with others to subject us to a **jurisdiction**[45] foreign to our constitution, and unacknowledged by our laws..."

The Treaty of Paris

㉔The Americans suffered severe setbacks for months after independence was declared. By December, Washington's forces were nearing collapse, as supplies and promised aid failed to come. In the early morning hours of December 26, Washington's troops surprised the garrison at Trenton, taking more than 900 prisoners. A week later, on January 3, 1777, Washington attacked the British at Princeton, regaining most of the territory formally occupied by the British. The victories at Trenton and Princeton revived **flagging**[46] American spirits.

㉕In July, 1780, France's Louis XVI sent to America a force of 6,000 men. In addition, the French fleet harassed British shipping and prevented supply of British forces. Finally, on October 19, 1781, the army of 8,000 British soldiers surrendered.

㉖On September 3, 1783, Great Britain and its former colonies signed the Treaty of Paris which acknowledged the independence, freedom and **sovereignty**⁴⁷ of the 13 former colonies. The **fledgling**⁴⁸ colonies had finally become "free and independent states." The task of uniting a nation yet remained.

Additional Material

(1,448 words)

Notes to the Passage

1. Royal Proclamation 皇家宣言
2. high-handed 高压的
3. extract 索取，榨取
4. revenue stamp 印花税票
5. lease 租契
6. bear... on 对……有影响
7. articulate 表达力强的
8. clergyman 牧师
9. constitutionally 按照宪法
10. legislature 立法机关
11. manifest 明显的
12. subvert 颠覆；破坏
13. repeal 撤消，废除
14. make do with 凑合着用
15. homespun 自己家里纺的
16. radical 激进分子
17. agitate 鼓动；煽动
18. Mohawk Indian 莫霍克印第安人
19. unanimously 一致地
20. vandalism 蓄意破坏
21. insurgent 起义的，反叛的
22. bring... into line 使……一致
23. coercive 强制的
24. dilemma 窘境；进退两难
25. unanimity 一致
26. radicalism 激进主义

27. keynote speech（在政治集会等场合作的）定调子的主要发言，基调演说
28. boycott（联合）抵制
29. mobilize 调动，动员
30. petition 请愿
31. Philadelphia Quaker 费城贵格会教徒，公谊会教徒
32. The die is now cast. 骰子已经抛出。
33. confiscate 没收
34. munition 军火
35. disperse 散开
36. casualty 伤亡
37. militiaman 民兵
38. Middlesex（马萨诸塞州的）米德尔塞克斯县
39. resound 引起反响
40. hereditary monarchy 世袭君主制
41. crowned 戴着皇冠的
42. ruffian 流氓
43. tyrannical 暴君的，专制的
44. outworn 陈腐的
45. jurisdiction 司法
46. flagging 萎靡不振的
47. sovereignty 主权
48. fledgling 新成立的

Reading Exercise

Directions: *After you read the passage, answer the following questions or complete the sentences with the information you get from the passage.*

1. Why did the colonies want to claim new land? _____

    A. Because a larger population needed some place to settle.

    B. Because the British Crown wanted to stop westward expansion.

    C. Because they wanted more freedom from British control.

    D. Because Britain was trying to organize the new system.

2. A stronger central British government would _____.

    A. have a king and a jurisdiction by American laws

    B. allow the formation of new colonies

    C. be a government based on popular consent

    D. come at the expense of colonial self-government

3. What was the result of the "Coercive or Intolerable Acts"? _____

    A. They brought economic disaster to Boston and other sea ports.

    B. They subdued and isolated Massachusetts as Parliament intended.

    C. They united Massachusetts and other colonies.

    D. They were finally repealed like the "Stamp Act."

4. Delegates at the First Continental Congress wanted to appear _____.

    A. united but moderate   B. radical and independent

    C. resolute and aggressive   D. peaceful but defensive

5. Who fired "the shot heard round the world"? _____

    A. Major John Pitcairn.   B. The British troops.

    C. The Minutemen.   D. Not stated.

6. What is the color of the uniform of British soldiers? _____

    A. Blue.   B. Red.   C. Green.   D. Not mentioned.

7. The purpose of the Second Continental Congress was to _____.

    A. appoint Washington as commander-in-chief of the American forces

    B. decide whether to go to war with Britain

    C. mobilize American forces into action

    D. defend Lexington and Concord

8. What was the main idea of Thomas Paine's *Pamphlet*? _____

    A. Attacking the idea of hereditary monarchy.

    B. Praising the worth of honest men to a society.

    C. Letting people know the two choices they were facing.

    D. Popularizing John Locke's principles of a nation.

9. The battles at Trenton and Princeton were vital because _____.

    A. they boosted the morale of colonial soldiers

    B. they allowed the colonial troops time to recover

    C. they cut off the supplies and aid of British armies

    D. they cleared the way for Washington's troops

Part D Speaking Activities

1. Interpret "All Men Are Created Equal"

Directions: *The most famous sentence in the Declaration of Independence is: "We hold these truths to be self-evident, that all men are created equal, that they are endowed by their Creator with certain unalienable Rights, that among these are Life, Liberty and the pursuit of Happiness."*

Discuss what the sentence "all men are created equal" might mean for different people:

A. For Thomas Jefferson, who wrote the Declaration (he owned slaves himself)

B. For Abraham Lincoln when he campaigned for presidency

C. For Martin Luther King

2. Translate the American Anthem

Directions:

Step 1   *Translate the first stanza of "Star-Spangled Banner" into Chinese. Compare your version with that of other students. Then get a recommended version from your teacher.*

> Oh, say can you see by the dawn's early light
> What so proudly we hailed at the twilight's last gleaming?
> Whose broad stripes and bright stars thru the perilous (危险的) fight,
> O'er the ramparts (防御土墙) we watched were so gallantly (勇敢地) streaming?
> And the rocket's red glare, the bombs bursting in air,
> Gave proof through the night that our flag was still there.
> Oh, say does that star-spangled banner yet wave
> O'er the land of the free and the home of the brave?

Notes:

thru = through   O'er = Over

Step 2   *Singing the national anthem is a way to cultivate patriotism in the citizens. What other ways do you think can cultivate patriotism?*

3. The Greatest Hero in the US History

Directions: *Work in groups.*

Step 1   *Talk about a great hero in the US history.*

Step 2   *Discuss what qualities are embodied in those national heroes.*

4. Slavery in the United States

Directions: *Work in groups to discuss how slavery developed in the United States. You may search online for relevant information. After the discussion, write a 300-word essay on the topic.*

Chapter 3

Education

Part A　Preview

A Quiz on the US Education

Directions: *Answer the following questions with as much detail as you can.*

1. When does the school year usually begin in the US and when does it end?

_____

2. What are the common school holidays in the US?

_____

3. What is the ratio of American students who attend public schools (schools supported by American taxpayers) to those who attend private schools, and to those who attend homeschools?

_____

4. What is SAT and what is ACT?

_____

5. What is ETS and what language tests does it provide to non-native speakers?

_____

6. What are the Ivy League schools? Can you name them?

_____

7. Generally, there are four kinds of institutions of higher learning in the US. They are _____, _____, _____ and _____.

8. All the US universities have their own emblems. Match the university with its emblem.

(1) _____   (2) _____   (3) _____   (4) _____

A. Harvard   B. Brown   C. Yale   D. Columbia

9. How many institutions of higher learning are there in the US?

A. About 1,700.   B. About 2,700.   C. About 3,700.

10. What percentage of Americans over the age of 25 are college graduates?

A. About 15%.   B. About 25%.   C. About 35%.

11. What do the following abbreviations stand for?

BS _____   BA _____

MS _____   MA _____

PhD _____

Part B   Listening

Scan and Listen

Harvard University

Vocabulary in the Listening

congress 国会	check out 登记借出
burn to ashes 烧成灰烬	erect a statue 竖立雕像
expel 驱逐，开除	violate 违反
artifact 人工制品	

Directions: *Listen to the passage on the history of Harvard University and fill in the missing information. You may listen again to check your answers.*

1. The number of new students Harvard admits a year is only _____.

2. We learn from the passage that Harvard University Library is the second largest in the US, next only to _____.

3. Two interesting things about Harvard are:

   (1) The statue of John Harvard has nothing to do with John Harvard, but is only a _____ of him.

   (2) The student who _____ in the 1764 fire was expelled from the university.

Part C　Reading for Information

Education in the United states

①Education in the United States is provided mainly by the government, with control and funding coming from three levels: federal, state, and local.

②The age for beginning school is **mandated**[1] by state law and therefore varies slightly from state to state, but in general children are required to begin school with a one-year kindergarten class during the year in which they turn 4 or 5. They are required to continue attending school until the age of 16 to 18, depending on the state. Students may attend public schools, private schools, or homeschools.

Preschool[2]

③There are no **mandatory**[3] public prekindergarten in the United States. The federal government funds the **Head Start**[4] preschool program for children of low-income families, but most families are on their own with regard to finding a preschool.

④In the large cities, there are sometimes preschools catering to the children of the wealthy. Because some upper-class families see these schools as the first step toward the Ivy League, there are even counselors who specialize in assisting parents and their **toddlers**[5] through the preschool admissions process.

Elementary School

⑤Elementary school, also known as grade school or grammar school, is a school of kindergarten through fifth grade (or up to sixth grade), where basic subjects are taught.

⑥Public elementary school teachers typically instruct between twenty and thirty students of diverse learning needs. At times an individual school district **identifies areas of need**[6] within the curriculum. Teachers and advisory administrators form committees to develop supplemental materials to support learning and identify **enrichment**[7] for textbooks. Many school districts post information about the curriculum and supplemental materials on websites for public access.

⑦Elementary school teachers are trained with emphases on human **cognitive**[8] and psychological development and the principles of curriculum development and instruction earning either a Bachelor's or Master's Degree in Early Childhood and Elementary Education. **Certification**[9] standards for teachers are determined by individual states, with individual colleges and universities determining the **rigor**[10] of the college education provided for future teachers. Some states require content area tests as well as instructional skills tests to be certified as a teacher within that state. Most states have predetermined the number of minutes that will be taught within a given content area.

Junior and Senior High School

⑧Junior high school usually includes grades seven and eight. In some locations, junior high school includes grade nine only, allowing students to adjust to a high school environment. Middle school is often used instead of junior high school when **demographic factors**[11] increase the number of younger students. At this time, students are given more independence in choosing their own classes. Starting in ninth grade, grades become part of a student's official **transcript**[12]. Future employers or colleges may want to see steady improvement in grades and a good attendance record on the official transcript. Therefore, students are encouraged to take much more responsibility for their education.

⑨Generally, at the high school level, students take a broad variety of classes without special emphasis on any particular subject. Curricula vary widely in quality and rigidity. The typical minimum course sequences that one must take in order to obtain a high school diploma are: Science (usually two years minimum), Mathematics (usually two years minimum), English (usually four years minimum), Social Science (usually three years minimum), and Physical education (at least one year). They are not indicative of the necessary minimum courses or course rigor required for attending college in the United States.

⑩Many high schools offer a wide variety of elective courses, although the availability of such courses depends upon each particular school's financial resources and desired curriculum emphases. Common types of electives include: **visual arts**[13], performing arts, technology education, computers, athletics, publishing, and foreign languages.

⑪Many high schools also provide **Advanced Placement (AP)**[14] or **International Baccalaureate (IB)**[15] courses. These are special forms of **honors classes**[16] where the curriculum is supposed to be more challenging than standard courses. AP or IB courses are usually taken during the 11th or 12th grade of high school, either as a replacement for a typical required course (e.g., taking AP

US History as a replacement for standard US History), a continuation of a subject (e.g., taking AP Biology in the 12th grade, after completing Biology in the 11th grade), or a completely new field of study (e.g., AP Economics or AP Computer Science).

College and University

⑫Post-secondary education in the United States is known as college or university and commonly consists of four years of study at an **institution of higher learning**[17]. The four undergraduate grades are commonly called freshman, sophomore, junior, and senior years. Students traditionally apply to receive admission into college, with varying difficulties of entrance. Schools differ in their competitiveness and reputation; generally, the most

prestigious schools are private, rather than public. Admissions criteria involve the rigor and grades earned in high school courses taken, the students' GPA, **class ranking**[18], and standardized test scores (such as the SAT or the ACT tests). Most colleges also consider additional subjective factors such as a **commitment to extracurricular activities**[19], a personal essay, and an interview.

⑬Some students choose to attend a community college for two years prior to further study at another college or university. In most states, community colleges are operated either by a division of the state university or by local special districts subject to guidance from a state agency. Those seeking to continue their education may later transfer to a four-year college or university. Some community colleges have automatic enrollment agreements with local four-year colleges, where the community college provides the first two years of study and the university provides the remaining years of study, sometimes all on one campus. The community college awards **Associate of Arts**[20] (AA) or **Associate of Science**[21] (AS) degree, and the university awards the bachelor's and master's degrees.

⑭Graduate study leads to a more advanced degree, which could be a Master of Arts (MA), Master of Science (MS), Master of Business Administration (MBA), or Master of Education (MEd), and Master of Fine Arts (MFA). After additional years of study and sometimes **in conjunction with**[22] the completion of a master's degree, students may earn a Doctor of Philosophy (PhD) or other doctoral degree, such as Doctor of Arts, Doctor of Education. Some programs, such as medicine, have formal **apprenticeship**[23] procedures like **residency**[24] and **internship**[25] which must be completed before one is considered to be fully trained. Other professional programs like law and business have no formal apprenticeship requirements, although law school graduates must take the bar exam in nearly all states in order to legally practice law.

⑮Entrance into graduate programs usually depends upon a student's undergraduate academic performance or professional experience as well as their score on a standardized entrance exam like the Graduate Record Examination, the Medical College Admissions Test (MCAT), or the Law School Admissions Test (LSAT). Many graduate and law schools do not require experience after earning a bachelor's degree to enter their programs; however, business school candidates are usually required to gain a few years of professional work experience. Only 8.9 percent of students ever receive postgraduate degrees, and most, after obtaining their bachelor's degree, proceed directly into the workforce.

⑯The vast majority of students (up to 70 percent) lack the financial resources to **pay tuition up front**[26] and must rely on student loans and scholarships from their university, the federal government, or a private lender. Because each state supports its own university system with state taxes, most public universities charge much higher rates for out-of-state students.

⑰Annual undergraduate tuition varies widely from state to state. A typical year's tuition at a public university (for residents of the state) usually ranges from $6,000 to $15,000. Tuition for out-of-state students is comparable to private school prices, although students can generally get state residency after their first year. Private schools are typically much higher. Depending upon the type of school and program, annual graduate program tuition can vary from $15,000 to as high as $40,000. Note that these prices do not include living expenses (rent, room/board, etc.) or additional fees that schools add on such as "activities fees" or health insurance. These fees, especially room and board, can range from $6,000 to $12,000 per academic year.

Additional Material

(1,361 words)

Notes to the Passage

1. mandate 批准
2. preschool 学龄前的
3. mandatory 强制的
4. Head Start: a program of the United States Department of Health and Human Services that provides comprehensive education, health, nutrition, and parent involvement services to low-income children and their families 开端计划
5. toddler 学步的小孩；蹒跚行走者
6. identify areas of need 确定学习范围/内容
7. enrichment 添加的内容
8. cognitive 认知的
9. certification 证明；证书
10. rigor 严密性，严谨
11. demographic factors 人口因素
12. transcript 学生成绩报告单
13. visual arts 视觉艺术
14. Advanced Placement (AP): a three-year sequence of course work in a specific subject equivalent to a first year college course. A student who achieves a 4 or 5 is usually permitted to skip the corresponding course as a freshman in college. 预修课程
15. International Baccalaureate (IB): a comprehensive curriculum designed to prepare students for liberal arts education at the college level. Students whose main goal is preparation for either a career with an international perspective or college in another country may prefer IB because of its recognition at overseas universities. 国际文凭课程

16. honors class 优等班

17. institution of higher learning 高等学府

18. class ranking 班级排名

19. commitment to extracurricular activities 参与课外活动

20. associate of arts 准文学学士

21. associate of science 准理学学士

22. in conjunction with 与……相结合

23. apprenticeship 见习期

24. residency 住院实习

25. internship 实习生的职位；见习期

26. pay tuition up front 提前支付学费

Reading Exercise

Directions: *After you read the passage, answer the following questions or complete the sentences with the information you get from the passage.*

1. The three levels of educational funding in America are _____, _____, and _____.

2. For schools at the elementary level, various names are used, like _____ school, _____ school, and _____ school.

3. Who is the Head Start preschool program intended for?

   A. Children of low-income families. B. Exceptional children.

   C. Children of upper-class families. D. Versatile children.

4. In order to qualify as an elementary teacher, one needs to have a degree in _____ and _____.

5. Good academic records from the 9th grade and up may help the student in _____ and _____.

6. If you do NOT want to receive more advanced training in high school, you may just take _____.

   A. an AP course B. an IB course C. a standard course

7. If you want to earn a bachelor's degree, you may go to _____.

   A. a community college B. a college

   C. a university D. all of the above

8. An example of a program which requires its candidate to complete residency and internship before one is considered as a qualified professional is _____.

9. Which program requires its graduates to take a qualifying exam before becoming practitioners? _____

10. The word board in "room and board" means _____.

    A. meals B. sports C. courses

Part D Speaking Activities

1. Take a Field Trip

Directions: *Work in groups. Suppose we are having some field trips. What places would you suggest as the destinations?*

2. Public or Private?

Directions: *Suppose you are the parent of a child ready to start school. You earn just enough to afford the child's education in a private school. Will you send your kid to a public school or a private one? Please make a decision based on the information given below.*

Public School	Private School
(90% of the children attend a public school)	(10% of the children attend a private school)
(1) Built around the belief that everyone is welcome and no child will be left behind; has special programs for students with particular needs.	(1) The students are determined through a selection process: does not have to accept children with special needs; extra resources may come at an additional cost.
(2) Free schooling; financial support by state and federal funding.	(2) Funded through tuition, donations and private grants; costs much more than the public school.
(3) A diversity of student backgrounds.	(3) A fairly homogenous student body with similar goals and interests.
(4) Average size: around 535 students. A disadvantage of larger classes: Teachers give less attention towards each individual student. An advantage: A larger student body could produce better programs and more diversity.	(4) 80% have fewer than 300 students. A disadvantage of smaller classes: a more limited set of programs and services. An advantage: a more controlled academic setting.
(5) Not religiously affiliated.	(5) Over two thirds have a religious affiliation.
(6) Offers a general program including math, English, reading, writing, science, history and physical education as well as music and art. What is taught is mandated by the state and learning is measured through state standardized tests.	(6) Can create their own curriculum and assessment systems, although many also choose to use standardized tests.
(7) Teachers are state certified or working toward certification.	(7) Teachers may not be required to have certification, and instead often have an undergraduate or graduate degree in the subject they teach.

3. Learn about American Culture

Directions: *How can Chinese students studying in the US learn more about the local community/ culture? Can you suggest some practical ways?*

4. Cultural Communication

Directions: *Suppose you are going to be an exchange student at an American university. You will bring some gifts with Chinese characteristics to your future American friends. What would you bring and why?*

5. Design a Photo Poster!

Directions: *If you were asked to design a photo poster showing the unique features of education in the US based on the reading text, what photos would you include?*

Chapter 4

Mass Media

Part A   Preview

Forms of Mass Media

Directions: *Look at the forms of mass media shown below and discuss with your partners which one you are most familiar with. Talk about its characteristics and its strengths and weaknesses compared with other forms.*

Book

Recording

Television

Radio

Newspaper

Magazine

Movie

Internet

Part B   Listening

Vocabulary in the Listening

Scan and Listen

intriguing 引起极大兴趣的	fleetingly 短暂地
Gannett Corporation 甘尼特报业集团	reproduction 复制
premium 加付款	

Directions: *Listen to the passage on the drawbacks of newspaper advertising and fill in the missing information. You may listen again to check your answers.*

The three drawbacks of newspaper advertising are: 1. _____, the challenge of 2. _____ and the constraints of using a 3. _____ medium.

The newspaper is usually 4. _____ at the end of the day and the ad won't have a 5. _____ to be read if the reader misses it.

It is up to the reader to 6. _____ what to read in a newspaper. If one newspaper article is not 7. _____ enough, the reader will turn to other articles or pages. It is 8. _____ for newspaper advertisements to get the reader's attention.

Though color ads appear in newspapers, their 9. _____ is not as good as those in magazines. Also, newspapers charge 10. _____ money for color ads.

Part C   Reading for Information

Understanding the Mass Media Industries

①Mass media in the United States consist of several types: newspaper, magazine, radio, television, movie, recording and book, and website. The use of the word *industries* **underscores**[1] the major goal of mass media in America—financial success. But the media are more than businesses: They are key institutions in society. They affect American's culture, buying habits and politics, and they are affected in turn by changes in American people's beliefs, tastes, interests and behaviors.

The Media as Business

②What you see, read and hear in the American mass media may **cajole**[2], entertain, inform, persuade, **provoke**[3] and even **perplex**[4] you. But to understand the American media, the first concept to understand is that the central force driving the media in America is the desire to make money: *American media are business, vast business*. The products of these businesses are information and entertainment.

③Other motives shape the media in America, of course: the desire to fulfill the public's need for information, to influence the country's governance, to **disseminate**[5] the country's culture, to offer entertainment and to provide **an outlet for**[6] artistic expression. But American media, above all, are profit-centered.

Who Owns the Media?

④In America, all of the media are privately owned except the public broadcasting service and national public radio, which survive on government support and private donations. The annual budget for public broadcasting, however, is less than 3 percent of the amount advertisers pay every year to support America's commercial media.

⑤Today the trend in the media industries, as in other American industries, is for media companies to cluster together in groups. This trend is called concentration of ownership and this concentration takes five different forms.

⑥*Chains*. Benjamin Franklin established America's first newspaper chain. This tradition was expanded by William Randolph Hearst in the 1930s. At their peak, Hearst newspapers accounted for nearly 14 percent of total nation6al daily circulation and nearly 25 percent of Sunday circulation. Today's US newspaper chain giant is Gannett, which owns *USA Today*[7] and hundreds of local media outlets in 46 states across the country. Broadcast companies also own chains of stations, called networks, and the Federal Communications Commission (FCC) regulates broadcast ownership.

⑦*Networks*. A network operates similarly to a newspaper chain. It is a collection of radio or television stations that offer programs during designated program times. The four major networks are ABC (American Broadcasting Company), NBC (National Broadcasting Company), CBS (Columbia Broadcasting Company) and Fox Broadcasting Company. NBC, the oldest network, was founded in the 1920s. This network and the two other old ones (CBS and ABC) were established to deliver radio programming across the country, and the network concept continued with the invention of television and Internet. Networks can have as many **affiliates**[8] as they want, but no network can have two affiliates in the same broadcast area. (Affiliates are stations that use network programming but that are owned by companies other than the networks.)

⑧*Cross-media ownership*. Many media companies own more than one type of media property: newspapers, magazines, radio and TV stations, for example. Gannett, which owns the largest chain of newspapers, also owns television and radio stations. The 1996 **merger**[9] of Capital Cities with ABC joined the programming power of Disney with the distribution system of the ABC television network. Rupert Murdoch's News Corporation owns newspapers, television stations, magazines, 20th Century Fox Film and Fox Broadcasting.

⑨ ***Conglomerates***[10]. When you go to the movies to watch a Columbia picture, you might not realize that Sony owns the film company. Sony is a conglomerate—a company that owns media companies as well as companies unrelated to the media business. Media properties can be attractive investments, but some conglomerate owners are unfamiliar with the **idiosyncrasies**[11] of the media industries.

⑩ ***Vertical integration.*** The most noticeable trend among today's media companies is vertical integration—an attempt by one company to control several related aspects of the media business at once, each part helping the other. Besides publishing magazines and books, Time Warner, for example, owns **Home Box Office (HBO)**[12], Warner movie studios, various cable TV systems throughout the Untied States and CNN as well.

⑪ To describe the financial status of today's media is also to talk about **acquisitions**[13]. The media are buying and selling each other in **unprecedented**[14] numbers and forming media groups to position themselves in the marketplace to maintain and increase their profits. Since 1986, all three original TV networks—NBC, CBS and ABC—have been bought by new owners.

⑫ The issue of media ownership is important. If only a few corporations direct the media industries in this country, the outlets for different political viewpoints and innovative ideas could be limited.

Who Pays for the Mass Media?

⑬ Most of the income that the American mass media industries collect comes directly from advertisers. Advertising directly supports newspapers, radio and television. (Subscribers pay only a small part of the cost of producing a newspaper.) Magazines receive more than half of their income from advertising and the other portion from subscriptions. Income for movies, recordings and books, of course, comes from direct purchases and ticket sales.

⑭ This means that most of the information and entertainment you receive from television, radio, newspapers and magazines, and websites in America is paid for by people who want to sell you products. You support the media industries indirectly by buying the products that advertisers sell.

⑮ You also pay for the media directly when you buy a book or a compact disc or go to a movie. This money buys equipment, **underwrites**[15] company research and expansion and pays stock **dividends**[16]. Advertisers and consumers are the financial foundation for American media industries.

How Does Each Media Industry Work?

⑯ Books, newspapers and magazines were America's only mass media for 250 years after the first American book was published in 1640. The first half of the 20th century brought four new media—movies, radio, recordings and television—in less than 50 years. To understand how this happened and where each medium fits in the mass media industries today, it is important to examine the individual characteristics of each medium.

⑰**Newspapers**. There are over 1,300 daily newspapers in the United States. There are more evening papers than morning papers, but the number of evening papers is declining. Papers that come out in the morning are growing in circulation, and papers that come out in the afternoon are shrinking. The number of weekly newspapers is also declining. Advertising makes up about two-thirds of the printed space in daily newspapers.

⑱**Magazines**. According to the Magazine Publishers of America, about 11,000 magazines are published in the United States. To maintain and increase profits, magazines are raising their subscription and single-copy prices and fighting to maintain their advertising income. The number of magazines people buy by subscription is going up, but newsstand sales are going down.

⑲**Book Publishing**. In 2020, the estimated net revenue of the US book publishing industry amounted to 25.71 billion US dollars. Retail bookstores in the United States account for about one-third of all money earned from book sales; the rest of the income comes from books that are sold through book clubs, in college stores, to libraries and to school districts for use in elementary and high schools.

⑳**Radio**. Radio is one of the most powerful media in the United States, with a weekly reach of around 82.5 percent among adults. There are over 15,000 radio stations in the US, all competing for a piece of this massive market. WTOP, a station operating out of Washington D.C. is the largest of its kind in the US, pulling in 62 million US dollars in yearly revenue. Online radio is also playing an increasing role in the radio market, with an estimated 974 minutes spent listening to online radio on a monthly basis in 2021.

㉑**Television**. TV is one of the most popular media in the United States, reaching a daily time spent of over four hours among adults. However, estimates suggest that the number of hours per day watching television will considerably decline and in 2023, adults will only spend two hours and 50 minutes in front of a TV. Younger people seem to spend significantly less time watching television than their older counterparts as alternative forms of entertainment have begun to greatly increase in popularity.

㉒**Movies**. In 2020, there were 5,798 cinema sites in the United States, a similar amount to the 5,773 recorded a decade earlier. However, a look at the figures during the mid to late 1990s shows that there has been a significant decrease in the number of cinema sites in the US, dropping from 7,744 in 1995 to just over 6,100 in 2005. With the increasing take-up of streaming services, leaked movie files available online and rising movie theater ticket prices, the gradually decreasing amount of cinema sites in the US is just one way in which the film industry and the act of going to the movies have changed.

㉓**Internet.** The Internet has provided a means for newspapers and other media organizations to deliver news and keep archives public. Revenue is generated through advertising or subscription payments.

㉔Overall, mass media industries in the United States are prospering. The division of profits is shifting, however, as different media industries expand and contract in the marketplace to respond to the audience. For example, if the population's interest shifts away from print media to video entertainment, fewer people will buy newspapers, magazines and books, which means that these industries could suffer. Understanding the implications of these changes is central to understanding the media as business.

Additional Material

(1,595 words)

Notes to the Passage

1. underscore 强调
2. cajole 哄骗
3. provoke 挑动，煽动
4. perplex 使困惑，使费解
5. an outlet for （感情、思想、精力发泄的）出路
6. disseminate 散布，传播
7. *USA Today*: *USA Today* is a national American daily newspaper published by the Gannett Company. It was founded by Allen "Al" Neuharth. *USA Today* is distributed in all 50 states in the US, the District of Columbia, Guam, Puerto Rico, Canada, and the United Kingdom. The newspaper is headquartered in the Tysons Corner, Virginia in Fairfax County. *USA Today* sells for US $2 in newsstands, although it is often found free at hotels and airports that distribute it to their customers; the paper is also free online. 《今日美国》

8. affiliate 联播台
9. merger （公司等的）合并
10. conglomerate 联合大企业
11. idiosyncrasy 特有的风格
12. Home Box Office: commonly referred to as HBO, a premium television programming subsidiary of Time Warner. It offers two 24-hour pay television services, HBO and Cinemax, to over 38 million US subscribers. HBO programming is broadcast into over 150 countries worldwide. 家庭影院频道，美国一个电视和流媒体服务提供商
13. acquisition （公司间的）收购
14. unprecedented 空前的
15. underwrite 承担经济责任，如支付特别费用等
16. dividend 红利；股息；回报

Reading Exercise

Directions: *Read the following statements and decide whether they are true or false according to the passage you have read. Put a "T" before a true statement and an "F" before a false statement.*

1. ☐ Media in the US mean not only entertainment, but also money.

2. ☐ Media play a crucial role in shaping people's political, social and cultural views in the US.

3. ☐ The major role of media in the US is to provide entertaining information for the public.

4. ☐ In the US, most of the large media companies are owned by the government.

5. ☐ Gannett is the largest newspaper publisher in the US.

6. ☐ With vertical integration, many media companies have expanded into fields which are not really related to their core businesses.

7. ☐ The author of the passage expresses his concern about the increasing concentration of ownership in the media industries.

8. ☐ The major source of income of the media industries is advertising.

9. ☐ Ticket sales account for the biggest part of the revenue of the movie industry.

10. ☐ Mass media industries in the US are prospering, though the division of profits is shifting.

Part D   Speaking Activities

1. Talk about Your Favorite Movie

Directions: *Work together with your partner and talk about your favorite movie. Describe the movie and explain why you like it.*

2. Pick One and Tell Why

Directions: *The following table contains some categories of TV programs and their examples. Pick one program you are most likely to watch and tell your partner why.*

Narrative Programs	Dramas	*NYPD Blue*
	Serials (soap operas)	*Dallas, This Is Us*
	Situational Comedies	*Friends, The Simpsons*
Nonnarrative Programs	Game Shows	*Family Feud, The Price Is Right, Jeopardy!*
	Reality Shows	*Survivor, America's Next Top Model*
	Talk Shows	*The Oprah Winfrey Show, Live with Kelly and Ryan*
	Public Affairs Shows	*Meet the Press*
	News	*Today* (NBC), *Good Morning America* (ABC), *60 Minutes* (CBS)

3. E-Books vs. Paper Books

Directions: *In 2020, e-book revenue in the United States reached 1.1 billion US dollars, up from 983.3 million in the previous year. Work in groups to discuss whether e-books will replace paper books in the future.*

4. Conduct a Survey

Directions: *Interview at least 3 classmates about their time and money spent on different media forms during an average week. Prepare a report based on your survey results and present it to the whole class.*

Time and Money Spent on Different Media Forms in a Week

	Time (Hours)	Money (Yuan)
Book		
Movie		
Newspaper		
Magazine		
Television		
Radio		

Chapter 5

Economy

Part A   Preview

Money in the US

Directions: *Let's play a matching game to see if you can tell what is on the US coins and bills. Be careful, though. Some may be used twice.*

Coins or Bills	Images
_____ 1 cent	1. John Kennedy
_____ 5 cents	2. Andrew Jackson / the White House
_____ 10 cents	3. Thomas Jefferson / Monticello (his home)
_____ 25 cents	4. Ulysses S. Grant / US Capitol
_____ 50 cents	5. Susan B. Anthony / the moon
_____ $1 (bill)	6. George Washington / the eagle
_____ $2	7. Alexander Hamilton / US Treasury Building
_____ $5	8. Benjamin Franklin / Independence Hall
_____ $10	9. Abraham Lincoln / the Lincoln Memorial
_____ $20	10. George Washington / the Seal of the United States
_____ $50	11. Thomas Jefferson / signing of the Declaration of Independence
_____ $100	12. Franklin D. Roosevelt / a torch and flowers

Part B Viewing

Scan and Watch

How Interest Rates Affect the US Markets

Vocabulary in the Viewing

federal funds rate 联邦基金利率
ripple effect 连锁反应
recession 经济衰退
bond 债券

Federal Reserve Board 美国联邦储备委员会
inflation 通货膨胀
inverse relationship 逆相关

Directions: *Watch the video about how interest rates affect the US markets and fill in the missing information.*

The federal funds rate is the rate that banks use to lend each other money. When the Federal Reserve Board changes that rate, a ripple effect 1. _____ throughout the economy. The Fed 2. _____ inflation indicators to manage inflation. When indicators rise more than 3% a year, the Fed raises the federal funds rate to keep rising prices under 3. _____. Higher interest rates mean higher borrowing costs, so consumers and businesses borrow less and spend less. Demand for goods and services drops and inflation falls. On the other hand, falling interest rates 4. _____ when the Fed lowers the federal funds rate. Borrowing becomes 5. _____ and people spend more. This can end a recession. Interest rates tend to 6. _____ consumer and business spending. When they're rising, consumers and businesses spend less, causing 7. _____ to fall and stock prices to drop. When rates fall, consumers and businesses spend more and stock prices rise. Bond prices and interest rates have an inverse relationship. As one increases, the other decreases. Governments and businesses raise money by selling bonds. But as interest rates move up, the costs of borrowing become more 8. _____. The demand for a lower-yield bond will drop, causing their prices to drop. Lower interest rates make it 9. _____ to borrow money. And many companies will issue new bonds to finance 10. _____. This causes the demand for higher-yielding bonds to increase and bond prices to climb higher.

Part C   Reading for Information

The US Economy

Basic Ingredients of the US Economy

①The first ingredient of a nation's economic system is its natural resources. The United States is rich in mineral resources and fertile farm soil, and it is blessed with a moderate climate. It also has extensive coastlines on both the Atlantic and Pacific Oceans, as well as on the Gulf of Mexico. Rivers flow from far within the continent, and the Great Lakes—five large, inland lakes along the US border with Canada—provide additional shipping access. These extensive waterways have helped shape the country's economic growth over the years and helped bind America's 50 individual states together in a single economic unit.

②The second ingredient is labor, which **converts**[1] natural resources into goods. The number of available workers and, more importantly, their productivity help determine the health of an economy. Throughout its history, the United States has experienced steady growth in the labor force, and that, in turn, has helped fuel almost constant economic expansion.

③The quality of available labor—how hard people are willing to work and how skilled they are— is at least as important to a country's economic success as the number of workers. Hard work and a strong emphasis on education, including technical and vocational training, contributed to America's economic success, as did a willingness to experiment and to change.

④Labor **mobility**[2] has likewise been important to the capacity of the American economy to adapt to changing conditions. When immigrants flooded labor markets on the East Coast, many workers moved inland, often to farmland waiting to be **tilled**[3]. Similarly, economic opportunities in industrial, northern cities attracted black Americans from southern farms in the first half of the 20th century.

⑤Labor-force quality continues to be an important issue. Today, Americans consider "human capital" a key to success in numerous modern, high-technology industries. As a result, government leaders and business officials increasingly stress the importance of education and training to develop workers with the kind of **nimble minds**[4] and adaptable skills needed in new industries such as computers and telecommunications.

⑥But natural resources and labor account for only part of an economic system. These resources must be organized and directed as efficiently as possible. In the American economy, managers, responding to signals from markets, perform this function. The traditional managerial structure in America is based on a top-down chain of command; authority flows from the chief executive in the boardroom, who makes sure that the entire business runs smoothly and efficiently, through various lower levels of management responsible for coordinating different parts of the enterprise, down to the **foreman**[5] on the shop floor. Numerous tasks are divided among different divisions and workers. In early 20th-century America, this specialization, or

division of labor[6], was said to reflect "scientific management" based on systematic analysis.

⑦Many enterprises continue to operate with this traditional structure, but others have taken changing views on management. Facing heightened global competition, American businesses are seeking more flexible organization structures, especially in high-technology industries that employ skilled workers and must develop, modify, and even **customize**[7] products rapidly. Excessive **hierarchy**[8] and division of labor increasingly are thought to **inhibit**[9] creativity. As a result, many companies have "flattened" their organizational structures, reduced the number of managers, and **delegated**[10] more authority to **interdisciplinary**[11] teams of workers.

⑧Before managers or teams of workers can produce anything, of course, they must be organized into business ventures. In the United States, the corporation has proved to be an effective device for accumulating the funds needed to launch a new business or to expand an existing one. The corporation is a voluntary association of owners, known as stockholders, who form a business enterprise governed by a complex set of rules and customs.

⑨Corporations must have financial resources to acquire the resources they need to produce goods or services. They raise the necessary capital largely by selling stocks (ownership shares in their assets) or bonds (long-term loans of money) to insurance companies, banks, pension funds, individuals, and other investors. Some institutions, especially banks, also lend money directly to corporations or other business enterprises. Federal and state governments have developed detailed rules and regulations to ensure the safety and soundness of this financial system and to foster the free flow of information so investors can make well-informed decisions.

⑩The gross domestic product (GDP) measures the total output of goods and services in a given year. But while it helps measure the economy's health, it does not **gauge**[12] every aspect of national well-being. GDP shows the market value of the goods and services an economy produces, but it does not weigh a nation's quality of life. And some important variables—personal happiness and security, for instance, or a clean environment and good health—are entirely beyond its scope.

A Mixed Economy: The Role of the Market

⑪The United States is said to have a mixed economy because privately owned businesses and government both play important roles. Indeed, some of the most enduring debates of American economic history focus on the relative roles of the public and private sectors.

⑫The American free enterprise system emphasizes private ownership. Private businesses produce most goods and services, and about two-thirds of the nation's total economic output goes to individuals for personal use (the remaining one-third is bought by government and business). The consumer role is so great, in fact, that the nation is sometimes characterized as having a "consumer economy."

⑬There are limits to free enterprise, however. Americans have always believed that some services are better performed by public rather than private enterprise. For instance, in the United States, government is primarily responsible for the administration of justice, education (although there are many private schools and training centers), the road system, social statistical reporting, and national defense. In addition, government often is asked to intervene in the economy to correct situations in which the price system does not work. It regulates "**natural monopolies**[13]," for example, and it uses **antitrust laws**[14] to control or break up other business combinations that become so powerful that they can **surmount**[15] market forces. Government also addresses issues beyond the reach of market forces. It provides welfare and unemployment benefits to people who cannot support themselves, either because they encounter problems in their personal lives or lose their jobs as a result of economic **upheaval**[16]; it pays much of the cost of medical care for the aged and those who live in poverty; it regulates private industry to limit air and water pollution; it provides low-cost loans to people who suffer losses as a result of natural disasters; and it has played the leading role in the exploration of space, which is too expensive for any private enterprise to handle.

⑭In this mixed economy, individuals can help guide the economy not only through the choices they make as consumers but through the votes they cast for officials who shape economic policy. In recent years, consumers have voiced concerns about product safety, environmental threats posed by certain industrial practices, and potential health risks citizens may face; government has responded by creating agencies to protect consumer interests and promote the general public welfare.

⑮The US economy has changed in other ways as well. The population and the labor force have shifted dramatically away from farms to cities, from fields to factories, and, above all, to service industries. In today's economy, the providers of personal and public services far outnumber producers of agricultural and manufactured goods. As the economy has grown more complex, statistics also reveal over the last century a sharp long-term trend away from self-employment toward working for others.

Additional Material

(1,260 words)

Notes to the Passage

1. convert 转变，变换
2. mobility 流动性
3. till 耕种，耕作
4. nimble mind 敏捷的思维
5. foreman 工头；领班
6. division of labor 劳动分工
7. customize 定做，定制
8. hierarchy 等级制度
9. inhibit 约束；抑制
10. delegate 授（权）给
11. interdisciplinary 跨学科的；跨领域的
12. gauge 测量；测定
13. natural monopoly 自然垄断
14. antitrust law 反垄断法
15. surmount 克服；越过
16. upheaval 动乱；剧变

Reading Exercise

Directions: *After you read the passage, discuss with your group members and answer the following questions with the information you get from the passage.*

1. What natural resources is the US rich in?

_____

2. Who are responsible for organizing and directing the natural and human resources?

_____

3. What is a corporation?

_____

4. What does GDP (gross domestic product) measure?

_____

5. Why is the US said to have a mixed economy?

_____

6. How do individuals help in a mixed economy?

_____

Part D   Speaking Activities

1. Company Profiles

Directions: *Work in pairs and share with each other what you know about an American company that is listed in Fortune 500. You may include its mission statement, major products, revenues, and market shares.*

2. A Quiz on Financial Knowledge

Directions: *Read the follow questions and discuss with your group members. Choose the best answer to each question.*

(1) If you went to college and earned a 4-year degree, how much more money could you expect to earn than if you only had a high school diploma?

    A. A little more; about 20% more.

    B. A lot more; about 70% more.

    C. About 10 times as much.

    D. No more; I would make about the same either way.

(2) If each of the following persons had the same amount of take-home pay, who would need the greatest amount of life insurance?

A. A young single woman with two young children.

B. A young single woman without children.

C. An elderly retired man with a wife who is also retired.

D. A young married man without children.

(3) Which of the following instruments is NOT typically associated with spending?

A. Cash. B. Credit card.

C. Debit card. D. Certificate of deposit.

(4) Which of the following statements is true?

A. Your bad loan payment record with one bank will not be considered if you apply to another bank for a loan.

B. If you missed a payment more than 2 years ago, it cannot be considered in a loan decision.

C. Banks and other lenders share the credit history of their borrowers with each other and are likely to know of any loan payments that you have missed.

D. People have so many loans that it is very unlikely that one bank will know your history with another bank.

(5) If you had a savings account at a bank, which of the following would be correct concerning the interest that you would earn on this account?

A. Sales tax may be charged on the interest that you earn.

B. You cannot earn interest until you pass your 18th birthday.

C. Earnings from savings account interest may not be taxed.

D. Income tax may be charged on the interest if your income is high enough.

(6) Inflation can cause difficulty in many ways. Which group would have the greatest problem during periods of high inflation that last several years?

A. Young couples with no children who both work.

B. Young working couples with children.

C. Older working couples saving for retirement.

D. Older people living on fixed retirement income.

(7) Under which of the following circumstances would it be financially beneficial to you to borrow money to buy something now and repay it with future income?

A. When some clothes you like go on sale.

B. When the interest on the loan is greater than the interest you get on your savings.

C. When you need to buy a car to get a much better paying job.

D. When you really need a week's vacation.

(8) Retirement income paid by a company is called _____.

A. rents and profits B. social security

C. 401k D. pension

(9) Kelly and Pete just had a baby. They received money as baby gifts and want to put it away for the baby's education. Which of the following tends to have the highest growth over periods of time as long as 18 years?

A. A US government savings bond.   B. A savings account.

C. A checking account.   D. Stocks.

(10) Which of the following best describes the primary sources of income for most people aged 20–35?

A. Profits from business.   B. Rents.

C. Dividends and interest.   D. Salaries, wages, tips.

3. Apply for a Credit Card

Directions: *Read the following scenario and role play with your group members.*

You are a telemarketing sales person for MBNA (a credit card company). You are calling potential customers to solicit applications for your credit card. You need to introduce your card and try to get them to apply for your MBNA card. You need the following information for the application: *full name, full address, phone number (both home and work), occupation, income level, prospect of future career, parents' income (if applicable).*

Don't forget to mention the advantages of your card over other cards, e.g. no annual fee, low interest rate, 24-hours emergency help, high credit line, special students' rate, etc.

4. Credit Card Use

Directions: *Discuss with your group members about the advantages and disadvantages of credit card use.*

Chapter 6 Work and Company Culture

Part A   Preview

Evaluate a Job Offer

Directions: *Discuss with your group members which three of the following will be your first considerations when you get a job offer. Give your reasons.*

salary	stock option	paid vacation
dental insurance	medical insurance	life insurance
optical care	pension plan	on-job training
working space	work uniform	work hours/shifts
location	your supervisor	company dining room
volunteer programs	fitness center	opportunity for advancement

Part B   Viewing

Scan and Watch

The Devil Wears Prada

Vocabulary in the Viewing

sack 解雇	facialist 脸部按摩师，美容师
rupture a disk 椎间盘突出	bagel 贝果；面包圈
gird your loins 准备行动	incompetence 无能
paunchy 大腹便便的	R. S. V. P. 尽快回复
sharp 整（指时刻）	dacquoise 蛋白酥皮奶油卷筒
torte （德国）果仁蛋糕	rhubarb compote 糖水大黄
paratrooper 伞兵	janitor 房屋管理员
skinny 极瘦的	glamorous 富有魅力的
headdress 头饰	Golden Nugget（美国拉斯维加斯的）金砖赌场

Directions: *Watch the beginning part of the video twice and answer the following questions. You may discuss with your partner.*

1. What is the name of the fashion magazine?

_____

2. Which university did Andy graduate from?

_____

3. Which position is Andy applying for?

_____

4. How did Andy get this interview with the magazine?

_____

5. Why did so many girls want to work for Miranda?

_____

6. What would be expected if Andy gets this position?

_____

_____

Part C   Reading for Information

Why Smart Women Still Don't Make It Up the Career Ladder

①*Though women have crowded out guys in classrooms, they still find themselves to be the outsiders in most career fields.*

②BROOKLYN, N. Y.—There are fewer men in **mortarboards**[1] these days, no doubt about it. According to **census**[2] data released last month, American women **surpassed**[3] men in both undergraduate and graduate degrees for the first time in history.

③But before we declare this happy ending of a feminist fairytale, we must look at the more **sinister**[4] **afterword**[5]. Between graduation stages and ***bona fide***[6] success in any number of fields, women simply disappear.

④While nearly half of law school grads are women, only about 16 percent of **equity partners**[7] at the top 200 largest law firms are women. Nearly one-third of MBAs are earned by women today, but corporate boards of Fortune 100 companies are still comprised of just 15 percent women. About half of those earning **MFAs**[8] are women, and yet about 23 percent of solo shows in New York galleries feature work done by women.

⑤**So what gives?**[9]

What Shuts Women Out?

⑥Though women have crowded out the guys in classrooms around the country, they still find themselves to be the outsiders in science labs, corporate firms, and **Chelsea**[10] galleries.

⑦Many studies confirm that until a minority group constitutes a critical mass—usually placed at 30 percent—it is in danger of conforming to the dominant culture, getting burned out by the heavyweight of **tokenization**[11] (as if one woman on the team could accurately represent one-half of the human population), or dropping out altogether.

⑧Every one of these fields where women are poorly represented has "pipeline issues"—places where the flow of smart, capable women gets **diverted**[12] because of poor infrastructure, irrelevant **red tape**[13], and a lack of **mentoring**[14] opportunities. Take architecture as an example. Women make up about 40 percent of graduates in the field, but thanks to the insanely lengthy and exploitative **licensure**[15] process, they are only about 10 percent of the 110,000 registered architects in the United States.

⑨Sometimes, as **Sylvia Ann Hewlett**[16] and others have argued, women lose their way in the dangerous maternal journey of "**on-ramping**[17]" and "off-ramping" (off-roading seems more accurate a metaphor in these tough economic times). But it's not adequate, or even accurate, to blame women's choice of mothering for their mysterious disappearance from these male-dominated fields. Is it so much to ask that we create work cultures that allow women (and men, for that matter) to work *and* **perpetuate**[18] the human race without losing their minds?

Women Aren't Socialized to Own Their Strengths

⑩But it's not just work/life policies and **crusty**[19] old office environments that are hindering women's career styles. It's unfashionable to admit this, but the truth is that women still have a confidence problem. As **Mary Pipher**[20] first argued in her bestselling 1995 book, *Reviving Ophelia*, when girls turn 13, societal and familial forces compel too many of them to exchange their healthy egos for a whole world of hurt and humility.

⑪The reasons for this shift are as layered and interrelated. In part, girls observe that women who adhere to stereotypically feminine traits—humility and self-sacrifice chief among them—seem to avoid the blinding spotlight and, thus, all the **alienation**[21] that can come from being an outspoken, self-possessed woman.

⑫On the other hand, and perhaps in an effort to avoid this kind of alienation, girls and women tend to explain their own success in far less individualistic ways than do boys and men. Former Facebook COO Sheryl Sandberg, giving the commencement address at Barnard College, touched on this: "Ask a woman why she did well on something, and she'll say, 'I got lucky. All of these great people helped me. I worked really hard.' Ask a man and he'll say or think, 'What a dumb question. I'm awesome.'"

Tears Instead of Negotiating

⑬As an advisory board member of The Op-Ed Project, an organization that aims to close the gender gap within public debate, I have seen roomfuls of highly educated and experienced women **downplay**[22] their own **credentials**[23]. I will never forget when one woman suggested that she had some knowledge of global development, but only after much pushing and poking admitted that she had a degree from Harvard, was the author of a critically-acclaimed book, and had led a highly successful grassroots movement for women's rights in **Nairobi**[24].

⑭It's not only owning our expertise that we **cower**[25] from, it's also negotiating on our own behalf. Linda Babcock and Sara Laschever, co-authors of *Women Don't Ask*, have studied this phenomenon extensively and concluded that "men use negotiation to get ahead and get what they want between two and nine times as often as women do."

Our Responsibility to Change Culture, Behaviors

⑮If you know a **visionary**[26] woman marching across a graduation stage this spring, you know a woman at serious risk of losing her hard-earned dream, whether she holds an MBA, a JD, or an M. Arch.

⑯All of us have a responsibility—men and women—to transform the American workplace so that it reflects the reality of working parents' lives, and socialize girls and women to proudly own their expertise in public and negotiate as fiercely as do their male peers.

⑰We have a moral obligation to mainstream what is best about stereotypically feminine behaviors—accountability, cooperation, humility—to break the myth of dishonest success, while also creating a world where women can claim their successes without being socially alienated. Otherwise, we're celebrating women's progress prematurely.

Additional Material

(917 words)

Notes to the Passage

1. motarboard 学位帽
2. census （官方的）调查，统计
3. surpass 超过，优于
4. sinister 险恶的；不祥的
5. afterword 编后记；跋
6. *bona fide* 真实的
7. equity partner 股权合作伙伴
8. MFA（Master of Fine Arts）艺术硕士
9. What gives? 发生了什么事情？
10. Chelsea 切尔西（伦敦泰晤士河北岸一个时尚区）

11. tokenization 象征化
12. divert 转向，改变
13. red tape 繁文缛节
14. mentor 指导
15. licensure 发执照
16. Sylvia Ann Hewlett: an economist, consultant, lecturer, and expert on gender and workplace issues 西尔维亚·安·休利特（美国经济学者，被评为"当代影响力商业思想家50人之一"）
17. on-ramping 上斜坡

18. perpetuate 延续
19. crusty 易怒的
20. Mary Elizabeth Pipher: an American clinical psychologist and author 玛莉·伊丽莎白·派佛（美国知名心理学家和作家）

21. alienation 疏远
22. downplay 贬低
23. credential 证书；资历
24. Nairobi 内罗毕（肯尼亚首都）
25. cower 畏缩；退缩
26. visionary 具有或显示出远见或智慧的

Reading Exercise

Directions: *Read the following statements and decide whether they are true or false according to the passage you have read. Put a "T" before a true statement and an "F" before a false statement.*

_____ 1. The number of male undergraduate students is larger than that of female students in the US.

_____ 2. Women have less career success than men after college.

_____ 3. About 60 percent of equity partners at the top 200 large law firms are female.

_____ 4. Only about ten percent of the 110,000 registered architects in the US are women.

_____ 5. Women should blame themselves for disappearing from career fields because they insist on being mothers.

_____ 6. Some women tend to explain their success in much less individualistic ways than men.

_____ 7. It is everyone's responsibility to transform the American workplace to reflect the reality of working parents' lives.

Part D   Speaking Activities

1. An Ideal Job

Directions: *Work with your partner and tell each other your ideal job after graduation. Discuss your strengths and weaknesses in securing your ideal job.*

2. A Job Description

Directions: *Read the following job description for a hotel receptionist and tell your partner whether you are qualified for the position and whether you will apply for the position. Give your reasons.*

JOB TITLE: Hotel Reception Clerk

General Responsibilities:

greeting guests; answering questions; responding to requests; obtaining or confirming room requirements; assigning rooms; obtaining information and signatures; issuing door cards; verifying credit cards or obtaining cash; showing room locations on hotel map; receiving and transmitting messages, mail, facsimiles, packages; etc.

Essential Functions:

(1) Welcomes hotel guests: greeting guests; answering questions; responding to requests.

(2) Registers hotel guests: obtaining or confirming room requirements; verifying pre-registration; assigning rooms; obtaining information and signatures; issuing door cards.

(3) Establishes guest credit: verifying credit cards or obtaining cash.

(4) Directs guests to hotel rooms: showing room locations on hotel map; calling bellhop.

(5) Conveys messages and deliveries to guests: receiving and transmitting messages, mail, facsimiles, packages.

(6) Provides information to guests: answering inquiries regarding hotel and other services guests may require, such as entertainment, shopping, business, and travel.

(7) Maintains hotel records: entering room and guest account data.

(8) Makes hotel and other reservations: entering or telephoning requirements; checking availability; confirming requirements.

(9) Secures guest valuables: placing valuables in safe deposit box.

(10) Contributes to guest services and hotel success: welcoming related, different, and new requests; helping others accomplish job results.

Other Skills Required:

Languages: English and Chinese (spoken and written)

Computer skills: Word, Excel, PPT

3. A Job Interview

Directions: *Read the following job description. Work in pairs to role play a job interview. One acts as an applicant and the other as a human resource manager.*

Customer Service Representatives, Newton Center, MA

The Customer Service Representatives support the marketing and sales efforts of Wandrian Inc. by providing information, answering phone inquiries and guiding customers in their buying decisions. Responsibilities include processing information requests, making reservations and supporting Wandrian Inc. programs in a timely and professional manner. This is an entry level position in a dynamic growing company with great opportunities and benefits.

Requirements:

- Sales and customer service focused.
- Energetic, personable and confident when talking to customers.
- Exceptional telephone sales skills.
- Computer skills such as Word, Excel and email.
- Excellent verbal and written communication skills.
- Organizational skills and strict attention to detail.
- Ability to take the initiative.
- Desire to work in a fast-paced environment.
- Flexible and team oriented.

Other considerations:

- Travel related background a plus!
- Knowledge of European Rail a plus!

Questions may include:

(1) How would you describe yourself?

(2) What specific goals, including those related to your occupation, have you established for your life?

(3) Have you had any work experience that has prepared you for this job position?

(4) How would you describe your organizational skills?

(5) What specific goals have you established for your career?

4. Give Your Advice

Directions: *Your friend Mark is not very happy these days. He came to you and complained that his fellow worker Jack had been promoted to the manager's position. Mark and Jack graduated from the same college in the same year and started to work for their company at the same time. Mark thought his boss was being unfair as Jack had been promoted while he had not. Have a conversation with Mark and give him some advice as to what he should do now.*

Chapter 7

Sports

Part A Preview

A Quiz on the American Sports

Directions: *Work in pairs and do the following quiz on the American sports.*

1. Which of the following is the championship game of professional football in the US?

    A. The Super Bowl.   B. The Rose Bowl.   C. The Orange Bowl.

2. How many teams are there on the National Football League?

    A. 30.   B. 32.   C. 28.

3. Which of the following is the sister of baseball?

    A. Handball.   B. Hardball.   C. Softball.

4. Which of the following basketball teams belongs to the Western Conference in NBA?

    A. Cavaliers.   B. Hornets.   C. Blazers.

5. Why is the Houston professional basketball team nicknamed as the "Rockets"?

    A. Because the NASA Mission Control Center is located there.

    B. Because rockets are launched into space there.

    C. Because rockets stand for a promising future.

6. Which of the following leagues includes teams from both the US and Canada?

    A. Football.   B. Baseball.   C. Ice hockey.

7. What are the "big three" sports in the US?

    A. Football, baseball and basketball.

    B. Baseball, basketball and soccer.

    C. Football, basketball and hockey.

8. Which of the following is a famous tennis player?

    A. Tiger Woods.   B. Pete Sampras.   C. Lance Armstrong.

9. Which of the following is usually an individual sport?

    A. Racquetball.   B. Rugby.   C. Paragliding.

10. Which of the following is of native North Americans' origin?

    A. Equestrian.   B. Lacrosse.   C. Curling.

Part B   Viewing

What Is the National Sport of the US?

Scan and Watch

Vocabulary in the Viewing

be poised to do sth. 随时准备做某事	topple 推翻；打倒
pastime 消遣；娱乐	NFL (National Football League) 美国职业橄榄球大联盟
populist 平民的	day-in-and-day-out 日常的
lethargic 昏睡的	back-and-forth 来来回回的
coordination 协调	athleticism 竞技
brutal 野蛮的	perverse 不合常情的
pastoral 田园牧歌式的	ascending 上升的

Directions: *Watch the video about a discussion on the American national sport and answer the following questions.*

1. Why is soccer in the news now?
_____.

2. What does Kornacki say about the popularity of soccer in the United States?
_____

3. What does Kornacki think is the national pastime of the United States?
_____

4. Why does Costas regard baseball as a pastime?
_____

5. What does Frank Deford think of baseball and football?
_____

6. What makes Mike think that football should not be frequently played?
_____

7. What does Mike say about basketball and hockey?
_____

8. What does Mike think about football?
_____

Part C Reading for Information

American Sports

①Sports in the United States play an indispensable role in the national culture. To many an American, sports have already become **part and parcel**[1] of their leisure life, and any weekend without some measure of participation, be it actual or emotional, would be hard to imagine. However, the sporting culture of the US is different from that of many other countries. Compared to any other nation, Americans prefer a unique set of sports. What's more, sports are organized differently in the US than in many other countries, with schools and colleges and universities playing an important role.

Team Sports

Football

②Football, known as the **gridiron**[2] outside of the US and Canada, attracts more television viewers, surging past baseball, America's most popular sport, in previous years. The 32-team National Football League (NFL) is the most popular and only major professional American football league. Its championship game, **the Super Bowl**[3], is watched by nearly half of US television households. Additional millions also watch college football throughout the autumn months, and some communities, particularly in rural areas, show great interest in their local high school football team. **Arena football**[4], a form of American football played in indoor arenas, has its own professional league, the **Arena Football League**[5], which attracts comparatively less attention, and is often considered **a niche sport**[6]. Nonetheless, it is regularly televised and several of its players have gone on to play in the NFL.

Baseball

③Baseball is the second most popular sport in the US, but due to its 162-game schedule, it attracts more ticket sales. It is still considered the "national pastime," as it has been a popular sport since the turn of the 20th century.

④**Major League Baseball**[7] teams play almost every day from April to October. Professional baseball began in the United States around 1865, and the National League was founded in 1876 as the first true major league. The **World Series**[8] is the championship series of Major League Baseball, the **culmination**[9] of the sport's postseason each October. It is played between the **pennant winner**[10] of the **American League**[11] and the pennant winner of the **National**

League[12]. The Series winner is determined through a **best-of-seven playoff**[13]. Baseball and its sister, softball, are also popular participatory sports in the US.

Basketball

⑤Basketball, invented in Springfield, Massachusetts, by Canadian physical education teacher James Naismith, is another popular sport, and is considered a **staple**[14] among the top 3 team sports. The **National Basketball Association**[15], more popularly known as the NBA, is the world's premier men's professional basketball league and one of the major professional sports leagues of North America. In late April, the NBA Playoffs begin. Eight teams in each **conference**[16] qualify for the playoffs. The **Dream Team**[17] was the unofficial nickname of the United States men's basketball team that won the gold medal at the 1992 Summer Olympics. Like football, basketball at both the college and high school levels is quite popular throughout the country. Every March, a 65-team, six-round, **single-elimination**[18] tournament determines the national champions of NCAA Division I (major universities) college basketball. There are also other national championship tournaments for NCAA Division II (mid-sized universities) and Division III (small no-athletic scholarship colleges). Most US states also crown state champions among their high schools.

Ice Hockey

⑥Ice hockey, universally referred to as hockey, is less popular than baseball, basketball and football, but is still considered a major sport. The **National Hockey League**[19] is the major professional league in North America, and 24 of its 30 teams are based in the United States; the other six are located in Canada. Always a cultural **mainstay**[20] in some northern areas, hockey has **gained tenuous footholds**[21] in regions like **the Carolinas**[22], **Tampa Bay**[23] (Florida) and **Dallas-Fort Worth**[24] (Texas) in recent years, as the National Hockey League pursued a policy of expansion. Recreational ice hockey on a wide scale, as well as hockey at the high school and college levels, is generally confined to hockey country, specifically New England and **the Great Lakes region**[25], but recreational leagues do exist in large- and medium-sized metropolitan areas throughout the United States.

Soccer

⑦Unlike in Europe, South America, Africa, and recently, Asia, soccer has historically had a small **following**[26] in the United States. Several attempts have been made to bring top-level competition to the United States, most recently **Major League Soccer**[27] (MLS). Since the 1980s, soccer participation at the recreational and scholastic levels has grown significantly and has fueled interest in the men's and women's national teams, as well as MLS, though **viewership**[28] levels for soccer matches still remain relatively low. Unlike most other team sports in the US, soccer is widely played by both men and women in the US, one factor in the pioneering success of the United States women's national soccer team.

Individual Sports

⑧Outside of team events, US athletes compete in sports such as boxing, golf, tennis, and track and field events. Golf is very popular in the US as a recreational activity, especially among business people. Track and field gets little mainstream attention from Americans apart from competition in the Olympic Games, while professional boxing has decreased in popularity over the past several decades. Tennis is played nationally at high school and college and America has given many of the all-time greats of the sport such as Bill Tilden, Jimmy Connors and Pete Sampras.

⑨Motor sports are widely popular in the United States, but Americans generally ignore major international series, such as **Formula One**[29] and **MotoGP**[30], in favor of home-grown racing series. Historically, **open-wheel racing**[31] was the most popular nationwide, with the **Indianapolis 500**[32] being unquestionably the most widely-followed race.

⑩Hunting and fishing are very popular in the US, especially in rural areas. Other popular outdoors activities in the country include hiking, mountain climbing and **kayaking**[33]. In winter, many Americans head to mountainous areas for skiing and snowboarding. Cycling has increased in popularity, fueled by the success of Texan cyclist **Lance Armstrong**[34].

The Organization of American Sports

Amateur Sports

⑪The extent in the United States to which sports are associated with secondary and **tertiary education**[35] is unique among nations. Millions of students participate in athletics programs operated by high schools and colleges. So-called student-athletes often receive scholarships to colleges in recognition of their athletic potential. Though student athletes may be held to significantly lower academic requirements than non-athletes at some universities, a minimum standard does exist.

⑫High school and college sports fill the developmental role that in many other countries would be the place of youth teams associated with clubs. Professional teams **draft**[36] top student athletes when they finish their education. Baseball and ice hockey operate minor league systems for players who have finished education but are not ready or good enough for the major leagues.

⑬Especially in basketball and football, high school and particularly college sports are followed with a **fervor**[37] equaling or exceeding that felt for professional sports; college football games can draw **six-digit**[38] crowds and, for **upper-tier**[39] schools, sports are a significant source of revenue.

Professional Sports

⑭There is no system of promotion and **relegation**[40] in American professional sports. Major sports leagues operate as associations of **franchises**[41]. The same 30–32 teams play in the league each year unless they move to another city or the league chooses to expand with new franchises.

⑮All American sports leagues use the same type of schedule. After the regular season, the 8–16 teams with the best records enter a playoff tournament leading to a championship series or game. American sports, except for soccer, have no equivalent to the cup competitions that run **concurrently**[42] with leagues in European sports. Even in the case of soccer, most casual soccer fans are unaware of the existence of a cup competition. Also, major-league professional teams in the US never play teams from other organizations in meaningful games, although NBA teams have played European teams in preseason exhibitions on a semi-regular basis.

⑯International competition is not as important in American sports as it is in the sporting culture of most other countries. Olympic ice-hockey and basketball tournaments do generate attention. The first international baseball tournament with top-level players, the **World Baseball Classic**[43], generated positive reviews after its **inaugural**[44] tournament in 2006.

(1,357 words)

Notes to the Passage

1. part and parcel 重要的部分
2. gridiron 橄榄球
3. the Super Bowl 超级碗（代表美国橄榄球的最高水平）
4. arena football 室内美式橄榄球
5. Arena Football League 室内美式橄榄球联盟
6. a niche sport 被束之高阁的运动；不够普及的运动
7. Major League Baseball 北美职业棒球大联盟
8. World Series 世界系列赛（美国棒球联盟和国家棒球联盟获胜队之间的比赛）
9. culmination 巅峰；顶点
10. pennant winner 美国职业棒球获胜队
11. American League 美国棒球联盟，北美职业棒球大联盟之一
12. National League 国家棒球联盟（北美职业棒球大联盟之一）
13. best-of-seven playoff 采用七战四胜制的季后赛
14. staple 主要部分
15. National Basketball Association 美国职业篮球联赛，简称美职篮（NBA）
16. conference 联盟（NBA分东西两大联盟）
17. Dream Team 梦之队
18. single-elimination 单淘汰赛制的
19. National Hockey League 北美职业冰球联盟
20. mainstay 唯一的依靠；支柱

21. gain tenuous footholds 稍稍开始立足
22. the Carolinas 南北卡罗来纳州，包括北卡罗来纳州（North Carolina）和南卡罗来纳州（South Carolina）
23. Tampa Bay （佛罗里达州的）坦帕湾
24. Dallas-Fort Worth （得克萨斯州的）达拉斯–沃斯堡地区
25. the Great Lakes region 五大湖区
26. following 支持者
27. Major League Soccer 美国职业足球大联盟
28. viewership 观众
29. Formula One 世界一级方程式锦标赛
30. MotoGP 世界摩托车锦标赛
31. open-wheel racing: An open-wheel car describes a car with the wheels outside the car's main body and, in most cases, one seat. Open-wheel cars contrast with street cars, stock cars, and touring cars, which have their wheels below the body or fenders. Open-wheel cars are usually built specifically for racing, frequently with a degree of sophistication unknown in other forms of motorsport. 开轮式赛车比赛
32. Indianapolis 500 印地安纳波利斯500赛车（一项传统的美式赛车比赛）
33. kayaking 皮艇
34. Lance Armstrong 兰斯·阿姆斯特朗（美国公路自行车赛职业车手）
35. tertiary education 高等教育
36. draft 挑选
37. fervor 热情
38. six-digit 六位数的
39. upper-tier 高级别的
40. relegation 降级
41. franchise 职业球队
42. concurrently 同时发生地
43. World Baseball Classic 世界棒球经典赛
44. inaugural 最早的；创始的

Reading Exercise

Directions: *After you read the passage, answer the following questions with the information you get from the passage.*

1. What is the Arena Football League?

_____

2. How can the Series winner of Major League Baseball be determined?

_____

3. If a college basketball team wants to win the national title, what must it do?

_____

4. Which sport is more popular in northern regions than in southern states?

_____

5. Where is recreational ice hockey widely played?

_____

6. What is the most important automobile racing event in the United States?

_____

7. Why, according to the passage, has cycling gained in popularity recently?

_____

8. What role do high school and college sports play in the US?

_____

9. How do major sports leagues in the US operate?

_____

10. What it the principal sporting culture in most countries?

_____

Part D　Speaking Activities

1. Interpret Sports-Related Terms

Directions: *Work in pairs. Interpret the following sports-related terms into English.*

(1) 国脚 _____	(2) 客场比赛 _____
(3) 五连冠 _____	(4) 体育道德 _____
(5) 头号种子 _____	(6) 卫冕冠军 _____
(7) 金牌得主 _____	(8) 组委会 _____
(9) 走步 _____	(10) 扣球手 _____
(11) 帽子戏法 _____	(12) 筑人墙 _____
(13) 发球 _____	(14) 双误（网球）_____
(15) 本垒打 _____	

2. Talk about Chinese Sports

Directions: *Work in groups to describe and comment on Chinese sports in as much detail as possible. The following aspects are just for your reference.*

● The sports system in China;
● The competitive sporting events in China.

Additional Material

3. Volunteer for the Olympic Games

Directions: *Suppose you are going to apply for the volunteer work for the Olympics. Give a 2-minute oral presentation to convince judges of your qualification as a volunteer for the Olympic Games.*

• Notes: A panel of judges, consisting of 5 students, are selected from the whole class first. They are required to ask the applicant questions to make sure that he or she is qualified. In the end, a total of 3 volunteers should be selected.

4. Give Your Views on Commercialization of Sports

Directions: *Work in groups to talk about whether the benefits of commercialization of sports outweigh the negative effects.*

Chapter 8

Leisure and Recreation

Part A   Preview

A Guessing Game

Directions: *The following are some pictures of leisure activities and their names. Match the picture with its name.*

Names of games:

a. Sightseeing

c. Scrabble

e. Hula hoops

g. Rope jumping

i.   London Bridge is falling down

k. Rafting

m. Rubik's cube

b. Tug of war

d. Jogging

f. Camping

h. Hopscotch

j. Top spinning

l. Snow-shoeing

n. Picnic

1.

2.

3.

4.

5.

6.

7.

8.

9.

10.

11.

12.

13.

14.

Write your answers here:

1. _____   2. _____   3. _____   4. _____
5. _____   6. _____   7. _____   8. _____
9. _____   10. _____   11. _____   12. _____
13. _____   14. _____

Part B   Viewing

Scan and Watch

How Americans Spend Their Weekends

Vocabulary in the Viewing

ground-breaking 具有开拓性的	dawn 开始出现
rewind 倒带，转回	get-away 逃跑
shuttle 往返运送	respondent 应答者
Blackberry 黑莓手机	buzz 发出嗡嗡声
dissolve 溶解；消除	blur 模糊
leash（牵狗的）皮带	slacker 偷懒的人
layoff 下岗	congressman 国会议员
mandatory 强制的	statistics 统计数据
yearn for 渴望	

Directions: *Watch the video about how Americans spend their weekends and answer the following questions.*

1. What is the main question raised in the video?
_____

2. Why does the video mention the Musotto family of Glendale, Arizona?
_____

3. Where do the Musotto family go on Saturday night?
_____

4. What are the examples of simple pleasures in the past?
_____

5. What do the people with kids between the ages of 9 and 17 do most of the weekends?
_____

6. What is the common wish expressed by the women interviewed?
_____

7. Besides shuttling kids, what else makes Americans busy on weekends?
_____

8. What is the main idea of the video?
_____

Part C   Reading for Information

Americans' Leisure and Recreation

Introduction

①In general, leisure time and recreation are available in a society or nation when financial resources and time are available. In the United States, economic growth and per capita income are among the highest in the world. For that reason, leisure time and recreation have developed to levels and types unimaginable to our parents, and our grandparents.

②Considering the evidence of the benefits of leisure and recreation, it is not surprising that many visitors to the US are surprised by the complexity and diversity of the use of leisure time. Many American recreational activities seem to be approached with a high degree of seriousness, planning, organization, and expense. Many Americans jog every day, or play tennis, **racquetball**[1], or bridge two or three times a week, or have some other regularly scheduled recreation. People interested in **astronomy**[2], bird watching, mushroom hunting, gardening, **quilting**[3], hiking can always find a group of like-minded people with whom to meet, learn, and practice or perform.

Benefits of Leisure

③Among the direct major benefits of leisure are: (1) physical and mental health, (2) economic development, (3) family **bonding**[4], (4) skills learning, (5) stress relief, (6) environmental awareness, and others which have been well **documented**[5] in research studies and project applications.

④To achieve the national health objective for increasing leisure-time physical activity, comprehensive public health efforts are needed to reduce the current increase of inactivity for all population age groups. Some of the suggested strategies include: (1) encouraging people to use stairs instead of elevators, (2) walking or riding a bicycle instead of using a car or other energy using transportation, (3) avoiding the use of needless labor-saving devices and appliances or tools, (4) organizing health education classes for the elderly, (5) increasing participation in physical activity and recreational sports of elderly and young people, (6) facilitating indoor activities, i.e., walking in malls, **workout rooms**[6] in businesses and schools, and (7) establishing and encouraging seasonal physical activities like gardening, winter outdoor sports, **raking**[7] and **bagging**[8] of leaves, and indoor or outdoor dancing.

Leisure Requirements by Ages

⑤The desire and need for leisure and recreational activity increases from the time of birth until physical maturity or adulthood. Parental or pre-school guidance is responsible for leisure and recreational activity in early years. Pre-school and elementary school students move from individual recreational activities to more organized, well supervised activities as they advance in grades. Free exercise on playgrounds gives way gradually to more group sports, dancing, drama and music. Physical education and recreation classes are often required, and this continues through high school and involves not only competitive team sports between schools and cities, but also the associated activities of **cheerleading**[9], vocal and instrumental groups, drama clubs, etc.

⑥A person's physical activity increases until it peaks at about age 20 to 35, depending on individual preferences, financial support, and time required for formal classroom study and homework. At the high school level, and certainly by college age, students tend to focus on selected activities which maintain fitness levels of the activity chosen. For some individuals, higher education begins the decline of leisure and recreational activity, sometimes by choice, and often because of the need for financial support for themselves, or for their families.

Types of Leisure and Recreation

⑦To name all of the types of games and recreational activities found in the US and elsewhere would take more room than we have available.

⑧There are various ways of classifying games, but the following is a common way used by scholars in the area of leisure and recreation: board & table games, including go, chess, Chinese checkers, **solitaire**[10], **dominoes**[11], cards, **scrabble**[12] etc.; street & playground games, including **hopscotch**[13], **shuttlecock**[14], **spinning tops**[15], jump ropes, **hula hoops**[16], **barrel rolling**[17], field & forest games, including **tug of war**[18], kites, nature study, and hiking; party & festival games, including **London Bridge**[19], **pinata**[20], **stilts**[21], **potato-sack racing**[22], and **darts**[23]; puzzles, tricks & **stunts**[24], including yo-yo, Rubik's cube, **African string puzzle**[25], match games, and bobbing for apples; individual & team sports such as golf, basketball, baseball, table tennis, badminton, tennis, swimming; yoga, skills & talents such as singing, debate, dancing, vocal and instrumental music, knitting, quiz shows and quiet times such as electronic games of all sorts, leisure reading, book clubs, **meditation**[26]; collection hobbies such as stamps, coins, knives, and many others. Most of us have engaged in some of these, or have seen them being played. There is no reason to doubt that new uses of leisure time may arise, even though they may be similar to many others that have occurred in human history.

The Cost of Leisure Activities

⑨Some leisure activities have a minimal cost, or very little cost as in walking, bird watching, etc., while others, such as racing cars or bicycles may be quite expensive. Most Americans prefer to have one or two activities for which they are willing to pay considerable sums of money, i.e. athletic club membership, golf equipment and club membership, etc., while most engage in a number of low cost activities such as hiking, nature studies, card playing, **marbles**[27], attending local high school sports, musical or drama events etc.

⑩In America recreation is a big business. Many common recreational activities require supplies and equipment that can be quite costly. **Recreational vehicles**[28] can cost as much as $35,000. The fashion industry has successfully persuaded many Americans that they must be properly dressed for jogging, playing tennis, skiing and so on. Fashionable outfits for these and other recreational activities can be surprisingly expensive.

⑪Most of middle-income families spend approximately $500 per year for leisure and playing activities, but some wealthy individuals, such as frequent gamblers, major sports fans, etc. spend in excess of $25,000 per year and demand comfort and expensive lodging, food, and services along with their recreation. Low-income families may spend as little as $50–100/year on leisure activities, and they may depend upon the school, church, or community to provide very low-cost participation. Certainly, the development of parks, trails, and natural areas has encouraged the inexpensive use of leisure time for many individuals and families. Generally speaking, golf and **yachting**[29] are associated with wealthier people, tennis with better-educated people, and outdoor sports (camping, fishing, hunting) with middle-class people. Those who bowl or square dance regularly are likely to represent lower-middle class.

Analysis of Leisure and Recreation

⑫One could, if wished, rank the use of leisure and recreational time in the US in a number of different ways. One could rate by cost per year, energy consumed or used in the process, level of skills required, or nearly any other type of grouping of sports and leisure activity. These ratings or measurements could be demonstrated or graphed, or data could be collected for a statistical analysis. At the top of the "energy used" scale one might place competitive sports such as basketball, track and field, football, wrestling, weight lifting, mountain climbing, etc. In the middle part of this scale could be hiking, fishing, hunting, and other activities which depend upon the amount of walking and the specific physical activity of casting (as in fly fishing, bait casting, deep sea fishing, etc.). At the lower part of the scale one could study the energy required for reading, watching TV or movies, meditation, idle conversation, etc. A continuum exists in energy requiring activities, financial costs, degree of stress relief, and any other types of analytical ranking of leisure use or sports.

⑬Such analytical studies have been used extensively in health examinations, design of exercise equipment, and dieting **regimes**[30]. There are of course other variables to be considered in such analysis, including age and gender differences, physical or emotional maturity, etc. It is almost certain that more leisure activities will appear as the comparable per capita income and time availability increases in human societies.

(1,295 words)

Notes to the Passage

1. racquetball 短网拍墙球，手球式墙球（比赛规则和场地都与有四面墙场地的墙手球相同，但击球用以皮带拴腕的短柄球拍，球较墙手球略大而软）
2. astronomy 天文学
3. quilting 缝被子，被上缝花纹的缝法
4. bond 建立亲密关系
5. document 用文件记录
6. workout room 健身房
7. rake 用耙子耙
8. bag 用袋子装
9. cheerleading 为……做拉拉队
10. solitaire 单人纸牌戏
11. dominoes 多米诺骨牌游戏
12. scrabble 一种英文拼字游戏，在拼盘上有很多小格，游戏双方各有很多字母块，根据一定的规则在拼盘上拼成单词
13. hopscotch 跳房子游戏
14. shuttlecock 羽毛球
15. spinning tops 抽陀螺
16. hula hoops 呼啦圈
17. barrel rolling 滚桶游戏
18. tug of war 拔河
19. London Bridge 伦敦桥游戏
20. pinata 皮纳塔（一种墨西哥传统游戏，用纸、陶或者布做成有趣的形象，外部用彩纸装饰，里面会装一些小玩具、糖果等，通常在举行仪式或者举办聚会的时候挂起来，参与者蒙着眼睛转几圈，然后挥棒将其敲碎。）
21. stilt 走高跷
22. potato-sack racing 人站在麻袋里往前跳跃的一种游戏
23. dart 飞镖
24. stunt 绝技
25. African string puzzle 非洲绳子谜
26. meditation 冥想
27. marbles 弹球游戏
28. recreational vehicle (or R.V., used for traveling and usually including provisions for sleeping, cooking, and bathing) 房车
29. yachting 帆船运动，游艇比赛，乘游艇出游
30. regime 同regimen, 养生之道，摄生法

Reading Exercise

Directions: *After you read the passage, tick (√) the ideas that are discussed in the passage.*

☐ 1. Economic development and leisure activities.

☐ 2. Ways of promoting people's activity.

☐ 3. Reasons for people's current inactivity.

☐ 4. The move from individual activity to group and organized activity.

☐ 5. The classification of leisure activities by scholars.

☐ 6. The difficulty of different games.

☐ 7. The association between activity cost and classes of people.

☐ 8. The grouping of leisure activities by age.

Part D Speaking Activities

1. What Are Your Favorite Activities?

Directions: *Work in groups to discuss the following questions.*

• Which activity (activities) mentioned in class have you never tried before? For those activities that you haven't tried, would you like to have a try? Why or why not?
• What are your favorite indoor and outdoor activities? State the reasons why you prefer these to others.

2. A Guessing Game

Directions: *Divide the class into 8 groups. Two groups (i.e. Group A and B) cooperate. So there should be four competing teams. Each member in Group A describes an activity in detail. But be sure not to mention the name of the activity. And any member in the other group (Group B) tries to guess the name of the activity. Then, the two groups take turns. The competing team that guesses the most activities within the time limit is the winner. Each member must take turns to describe an activity, but the guesser can be anyone in the other group. The guesser has THREE tries. After three tries, if he or she still fails to guess the activity, the activity will pass. Before the game starts, you will have about 2 minutes to prepare. Any repeated activity cannot be counted, so be sure to prepare more than one activity and listen carefully when others are describing or guessing. The time limit for each competing team is 4 minutes. So the whole game will take about 20 minutes. Draw lots to decide which group starts.*

3. Teach Others a New Game

Directions: *Teach others a new game. It can be an activity/game/magic show that you played while you were a kid or an activity/game/magic show people in your area play but others have no idea of.*

4. Chinese College Students' Favorite Ways to Spend Their Leisure Time

Directions: *Work in groups and design a questionnaire with about 8 questions. This questionnaire is intended to investigate what the Chinese college students' favorite ways to spend their leisure time are. You should have about 30 respondents. You may also include the gender into your survey, and compare the differences. After the survey, analyze your results and write a report entitled "Chinese College Students' Favorite Ways to Spend Their Leisure Time" with about 180 words and then present it orally in the class.*

Additional Material

Chapter 9

Music

Part A   Preview

Scan and Listen

A Quiz on Music Appreciation

Directions: *Listen to 5 songs on the recording and categorize each of them into one type of music as follows: folk music, R&B, jazz, hip-hop/rap, and country music.*

1. _____   2. _____   3. _____

4. _____   5. _____

Part B   Listening

Scan and Listen

What Is Live Streaming?

Vocabulary in the Listening

video streaming 视频流	decompress 解压缩
subscription 订阅	copyright 版权，著作权

Directions: *Listen to the passage on video streaming and fill in the missing information. You may listen again to check your answers.*

Video streaming is a continuous transmission of video and audio files from a server to a client, ultimately allowing people to view videos online without needing to 1. _____ them first. Data is sent in a compressed form over the Internet to an individual who then needs a player that will decompress the data. It sends video data to the user's 2. _____ and audio data to their speakers. Common video streaming applications include YouTube, Netflix or Disney plus, for example.

Video streams are usually sent from a pre-recorded video file, but they can also be distributed as part of a live broadcast 3. _____, like in live streaming platforms such as Twitch. Video streaming offers benefits like allowing users to watch content without needing to download it first, providing high 4. _____, sometimes up to 4K, 5. _____, ranging from free services to subscription services even cheaper than cable, and a 6. _____ of content. Users can stream TV shows, movies or any kind of user-generated content like blogs, tutorials or video game streams. However, users may also have to deal with some 7. _____ too, including slow connections which with interrupted and dropped streams create a 8. _____ experience; even buffering, which is when a video stream loads a few seconds ahead of time to avoid any hiccups, can't 9. _____ poor connectivity. Copyright issues, especially in user-generated content on YouTube and Twitch, where creators have to worry about including copyrighted content like music from appearing in their videos. And 10. _____ performing client devices. If your phone or computer is old or has too many processes running, video streams may slow or drop out.

Part C   Reading for Information

American Music

①**James Fenimore Cooper**[1], an early American writer, once said, "The Americans are almost ignorant of the art of music." If that was once true, you would never know it today. Most Americans—even those without a musical bone in their bodies—have a favorite style of music. Many people enjoy classical and folk music from around the world. But other popular music styles in America were "made in the USA," which have gained a global audience since the beginning of the 20th century.

Folk Music

②Folk music has no nameable origin. It's more tradition than entertainment. There are folk songs that date so far back that they can be considered oral histories. Certainly, in America, songs by traditional American folksingers like **Leadbelly**[2] and **Woody Guthrie**[3] tell stories that often don't even appear in history books.

③From its origins, folk music has been the music of the working class. It is community-focused and has rarely enjoyed commercial success. By definition, it is something anyone can understand and in which everyone is welcome to participate. Folk songs range in subject matter from war, work, civil rights, and economic hardship to nonsense, **satire**[4] and, of course, love songs.

④**From the onset of**[5] American history, folk music has shown up at times when the people needed it most. The earliest folk songs rose from slave fields as **spirituals**[6]: "Down by the Riverside," "We Shall Overcome," etc. These are songs about struggle and hardship, but are also full of hope. They sprang from the need of the worker to go to a place in her brain where she knew there was more to the world than the hardships she was facing at the time.

⑤American folk music has now begun to **swell**[7] again, as workers find themselves in a position of **nostalgia**[8]. Folk singers in New York, Boston, Austin and San Francisco have emerged with a new brand of music. **Alt-country**[9] has evolved over the past couple of decades. A new generation of **bluegrass**[10] bands has changed the name of the **genre**[11] to **newgrass**[12], thanks to bands like Nickel Creek, Railroad Earth, and Open Road. Folk festivals are thriving with younger audiences joining their parents' generation in celebrating folk singers/songwriters like Dar Williams, Greg Brown and Ani DiFranco.

⑥Folk singers may be of an **ilk**[13] that rarely **goes multi-platinum**[14], but their work truly **resonates**[15] with people of all walks of life, and their legacy is astounding.

Blues

⑦Blues is about tradition and personal expression. **At its core**[16], the blues has remained the same since its **inception**[17]. Most blues feature simple, usually **three-chord progressions**[18] and have simple structures that are open to endless **improvisations**[19], both lyrical and musical.

⑧The blues grew out of African spirituals and work songs. In the late 1800s, southern African Americans passed the songs down orally, and these collided with American folk and country from the Appalachians. New **hybrids**[20] appeared in each region, but all of the recorded blues from the early 1900s are distinguished by simple, rural **acoustic guitars**[21] and pianos.

⑨After World War II, the blues began to **fragment**[22], with some musicians holding on to acoustic traditions and others taking it to **jazzier**[23] territory. However, most **bluesmen**[24] followed Muddy Waters' lead and played the blues on electric instruments. From that point on, the blues continued to develop into new directions—particularly on electric instruments—or it has been preserved as an acoustic tradition.

R&B

⑩R&B, an abbreviation for rhythm and blues, which combines **soulful**[25] singing and a strong **backbeat**[26], was the most popular music created by and for African Americans between the end of World War II and the early 1960s. Such Georgia artists as Ray Charles, Little Richard, and James Brown rank among the most influential and innovative R&B performers.

⑪Surging employment during World War II accelerated the migration of the rural poor to cities and helped create a younger, more urban black audience. By 1946 the decade-long dominance of **swing music**[27] was fading, but the demand for exciting dance music remained. Early R&B artists broke away from the big band formula by typically performing in small **combos**[28] and emphasizing blues-style vocals and song structures. Saxophone and piano were still prominent, but electric guitar and **bass**[29] added volume and intensity, making the new sound ideal for radio and **jukeboxes**[30].

⑫No R&B performer has been more influential than singer and bandleader James Brown. Brought up in **Augusta**[31], Georgia, Brown became known as the hardest-working man in show business for his **relentless**[32] touring and explosive stage performances. His first hit was *Please, Please, Please* (1956). His million-selling *Live at the Apollo* album (1963) achieved **unprecedented**[33] success. Starting with *Papa's Got a Brand New Bag* and *I Got You (I Feel Good)* in 1965, Brown evolved a new, **funky**[34] style that emphasized intense rhythmic interplay between vocals, horns, guitar, and drums.

⑬The first contemporary R&B stars arose in the 1980s, with the **funk**[35]-influenced singer Prince, dance-pop star Michael Jackson, and a wave of female vocalists like Tina Turner and Whitney Houston. In the 2000s contemporary R&B has produced many of the country's biggest pop stars, including Mariah Carey, Usher and Christina Aguilera.

Rock & Roll

⑭Rock & roll is often used as a **generic term**[36], but its sound is rarely predictable. From the outset, when the early rockers merged country and blues, rock has been defined by its energy, rebellion and **catchy hooks**[37], but as the genre aged, it began to shed those very characteristics, placing equal emphasis on craftsmanship and **pushing the boundaries of**[38] the music. As a result, everything from Chuck Berry's pounding, three-chord rockers and the sweet harmonies of the Beatles to the soulful pleas of Otis Redding and the jarring, atonal white noise of Sonic Youth has been categorized as "rock." That's accurate—rock & roll had a specific sound and image for only a handful of years. For most of its life, rock has been fragmented, **spinning off**[39] new styles and variations every few years, from Brill Building pop and heavy metal to dance-pop and **grunge**[40]. And that's only natural for a genre that began its life as a fusion of styles.

Jazz

⑮Jazz has been called America's classical music, and for good reason. Along with the blues, its forefather, it is one of the first truly **indigenous**[41] music forms to develop in America. At the outset, jazz was dance music, performed by **swinging**[42] big bands. Soon, the dance elements faded into the background and improvisation became the key element of the music. As the genre evolved, the music split into a number of different styles, from the speedy, hard-hitting rhythms of **be-bop**[43] and the **laid-back**[44], mellow harmonies of cool jazz to the **jittery**[45], **atonal**[46] **forays**[47] of free jazz and the **earthy**[48] **grooves**[49] of soul jazz. What tied it all together was a foundation in the blues, a reliance on group interplay and unpredictable improvisation. Throughout the years, and in all the different styles, those are the qualities that defined jazz.

Rap

⑯Rap's **germination**[50] is sometimes attributed to the righteous street poetry of **the Last Poets**[51] and **the Watts Prophets**[52], but it didn't begin to take full shape—and earn its tag—until after **the Sugarhill Gang**[53] released *Rapper's Delight* in 1979. Since then, rap has spread from its New York **epicenter**[54] throughout the remainder of the US (with each region taking on its own specific flavor) and then to countless countries. Rap's core components are beats and rhymes, but that simplicity **belies**[55] the wide range of sounds that have sprung from them. Instrumentalists, a sampled **breakbeat**[56], or a drum machine can form the backbone of a track, while an arrangement can be spaciously spare or **chaotically**[57] dense, and a chorus can range from atonal shouting to a sweet melody.

Hip-Hop

⑰In the **terminology**[58] of rap music, hip-hop usually refers to the culture—**graffiti**[59]-spraying, **breakdancing**[60], and **turntablism**[61] in addition to rapping itself—surrounding the music. As a style, however, hip-hop refers to music created with those values in mind. Once rap had been around long enough to actually have a history, hip-hop groups began looking back to old-school figures including **MCs**[62] like Kurtis Blow and Whodini, and **DJs**[63] like Grandmaster Flash and Afrika Bambaataa. In fact, the latter's **Zulu Nation**[64] collective sprang up in the late 1980s around two of the most notable hip-hop artists, De La Soul and A Tribe Called Quest. With rap music's mainstream breakout during the 1990s, dozens of hip-hop artists pointed the way back to the old school, including underground rappers like Mos Def and Pharoahe Monch.

Country Music

⑱Country music is about tradition, yet its simple form lends itself to endless variations on similar themes. Like the blues—the two genres often share themes, melodies and songs—country is a simple music at its core. Most of its songs are built around three chords and a plain melody, but these forms are so basic that they allow for many different styles, from the **gritty**[65] sounds of **honky tonk**[66] to the jazzy improvisations of **Western Swing**[67].

⑲Country music grew out of American Southern folk music, both Appalachian and blues, and old-time country was simple and folky, with just guitars and **fiddles**[68]. As the genre progressed, old time music evolved into the rhythmic guitar-and-fiddle driven traditional country that became the foundation of modern country music, from honky tonk and Western Swing to the **pop-oriented**[69] **Countrypolitan**[70] and rock-inflected **Bakersfield Sound**[71].

Soul

⑳Soul music was the result of the urbanization and commercialization of rhythm and blues in the 1960s. Soul came to describe a number of R&B-based music styles. During the first part of the 1960s, soul music remained close to its R&B roots. However, musicians pushed the music in different directions; usually, different regions of America produced different kinds of soul. In urban centers like New York, Philadelphia, and Chicago, the music concentrated on vocal interplay and smooth productions. In Detroit, Motown concentrated on creating a pop-oriented sound that was **informed**[72] equally by gospel, R&B, and rock & roll. In the South, the music became harder and tougher, relying on **syncopated**[73] rhythms, raw vocals, and **blaring**[74] horns. All of these styles formed soul, which ruled the **black music charts**[75] throughout the 1960s and also frequently crossed over into the pop charts. At the end of the 1960s, soul began to **splinter**[76] apart, and other artists developed more sophisticated and, in some cases, more politically conscious varieties. Although soul music evolved, it never went away—not only did the music inform all of the R&B of the 1970s, 1980s, and 1990s, there were always pockets of musicians around the world that kept performing traditional soul.

Additional Material

(1,785 words)

Notes to the Passage

1. James Fenimore Cooper 詹姆斯·费尼莫尔·库珀（美国浪漫主义文学的先驱者和奠基人之一，其作品《拓荒者》（*The Pioneers*, 1823）、《最后的莫希干人》（*The Last of the Mohicans*, 1826）等蜚声世界

2. Leadbelly 列贝里（早期美国黑人民谣的记录者与创作者）

3. Woody Guthrie 伍迪·格思里（被称为美国民歌鼻祖）

4. satire 讽刺

5. from the onset of 从……开始

6. spiritual 圣歌（美国黑人所创的宗教民歌）

7. swell 发展；膨胀

8. nostalgia 怀旧；乡愁

9. alt-country 另类乡村音乐（alt在这里指的是alternative，意为"另类的，非主流的"）

10. bluegrass 蓝草音乐（一种复调乡土音乐，用未经扩音的弦乐器演奏）

11. genre 类型；流派

12. newgrass 新草乡村音乐（美国乡村音乐的一种）

13. ilk 种类，同类

14. go multi-platinum 成为多白金唱片（销量超过普通白金唱片两倍的唱片称为多白金唱片）

15. resonate （使）共鸣

16. at one's core 在本质上

17. inception 开端，开始

18. three-chord progression 三弦乐

19. improvisation 即兴表演

20. hybrid 混合物；结合体

21. acoustic guitar 原声吉他

22. fragment 瓦解；分裂

23. jazzy 有爵士特点的；奔放的

24. bluesman 演奏（或演唱）蓝调舞曲（或歌曲）的人

25. soulful 深情的，充满感情的

26. backbeat 基调强节奏（一种响亮、稳定、有摇滚乐特点的节拍）

27. swing music 摇摆舞音乐

28. combo 小型乐队

29. bass 低音乐器，特别是低音提琴

30. jukebox 投币式自动点唱机

31. Augusta 奥古斯塔（缅因州首府）

32. relentless 持续的,·不断的

33. unprecedented 空前的，史无前例的

34. funky 有强节奏、适于跳舞的

35. funk 放克乐（一种综合了爵士乐、布鲁斯歌曲和爵士灵歌特性的流行音乐，以多切分音的节奏和低沉、经常重复的低音线为特征）

36. generic term 通称

37. catchy hook 好听上口的主调或结尾重复

38. push the boundaries of 拓宽……的范围

39. spin off 分离出，独立出

40. grunge 油渍摇滚（有时也被称作西雅图之声，是一种隶属于独立摇滚的音乐流派，由朋克、重金属等发展演变而来）

41. indigenous 本土的

42. swinging 愉快活跃的；多姿多彩的

43. be-bop 一种爵士音乐（以节奏疯狂为特征）

44. laid-back 自由的；轻松悠闲的

45. jittery 神经质的；战战兢兢的

46. atonal 无调的

47. foray 涉足，尝试

48. earthy 朴实的

49. groove 节奏

50. germination 萌芽；发生

51. the Last Poets 最后的诗人（一乐队名，对说唱乐产生了重大影响）

52. the Watts Prophets 瓦特先知（一乐队名，对说唱乐产生了重大影响）

53. the Sugarhill Gang 糖山帮（一说唱乐队名）

54. epicenter 中心，震中

55. belie 掩饰

56. breakbeat 碎拍（相对于4/4拍的规律性，碎拍的曲子常有着切分拍，拍子之间也常带着小碎鼓）

57. chaotically 混乱地，无序地

58. terminology 术语学

59. graffiti 涂鸦

60. breakdancing 霹雳舞

61. turntablism 唱盘主义音乐

62. MC（master of ceremonies的缩写）司仪，节目主持人

63. DJ（disc jockey的缩写）（广播电台）流行音乐播音员；流行音乐节目主持人

64. Zulu Nation 祖鲁国家，由阿弗里卡·邦巴塔（Afrika Bambataa）于1973年在纽约创立，是一个有计划地推广各式黑人音乐文化的组织，纽约许多重量级的嘻哈艺人与团体都是这个组织的成员

65. gritty 砂砾般的；粗糙的

66. honky tonk 一种早期乡村音乐形式，由欧内斯特·塔布（Ernest Tubb）和汉克·威廉姆斯（Hank Williams）催生而来

67. Western Swing 西部摇摆乐风

68. fiddle 小提琴

69. pop-oriented 以流行音乐为导向的

70. Countrypolitan 都市乡村乐

71. Bakersfield Sound 贝克斯费尔德之声，20世纪50年代中后期发展起来的一个乡村音乐的流派

72. inform 赋特征于；渗透

73. syncopated 切分的

74. blaring 响亮的；刺耳的

75. black music chart 黑人音乐榜单

76. splinter 分裂；破裂

Reading Exercise

Directions: *After you read the passage, answer the following questions with the information you get from the passage.*

1. What are the themes of American folk songs?

_____

2. Why has folk music now started to thrive again?

_____

3. What are the essential characteristics of the blues?

_____

4. What did the blues originate from?

_____

5. What makes the new sound of R&B ideal for radio and jukeboxes?

_____

6. What have remained to be the characteristics of rock & roll since its inception?

_____

7. Why is jazz perceived as America's classical music?

_____

8. What are the core components of rap?

_____

9. What culture is embodied in hip-hop?

_____

10. What characteristics does soul have in Dallas?

_____

Part D   Speaking Activities

1. A Mock Interview with an American Musician

Step 1
Directions: *Each student collects information about an American musician, including his/her life, personality, music, concert, etc.*

Step 2
Directions: *Work in pairs. One student plays a role as the American musician while the other plays a role as a TV host interviewing the musician.*

2. Air Your Opinion

Directions: ***American Idol*** *is an annual American televised singing competition, which began its first season in June 11, 2002. The first season debuted without hype* （炒作，宣传） *as a summer replacement show. But now it has become a household program. In China, a wide range of similar shows have also gained popularity. Now discuss with each other your view on such programs from different perspectives.*

3. Entertaining Time: The Best Singer

Directions: *Each group is required to select at least one student as a representative, singing an English song. After the performance, the whole class votes for the best singer. The one who gets the most votes wins.*

Chapter 10

Social Problems

Part A   Preview

A Quiz on Social Problems in the US

Directions: *Look at the following pictures and find out about the social problems behind them.*

1. _____

2. _____

3. _____

4. _____

5. _____

6. _____

7. _____

8. _____

9. _____

Part B   Listening

Graffiti: Street Art or Vandalism?

Scan and Listen

Vocabulary in the Listening

graffiti 涂鸦
aka 也被称为
a correctional facility 教养所，监狱的一区
authorization 批准，授权
aesthetic 美感；审美观
vandalism（尤指对公共财产的）故意破坏

Prohibition era 美国禁酒时期（1920—1933年）
scrawl 潦草地写
deface 损坏……的外观（尤指乱涂、乱写）
canvas 画布
curate 策展

Exercise 1

Directions: *Listen to the passage on graffiti culture in America and fill in the missing information. You may listen again to check your answers.*

Although people have drawn images and written slogans in public spaces all over the world for centuries, graffiti culture in America began to (1) _____ in the 1920s, when Prohibition era gangsters began painting gang signs on trains to mark out their (2) _____. But it's Philadelphia-born Darryl McCray, aka Cornbread, that is generally (3) _____ as the godfather of graffiti as we know it today. In the mid-1960s, a teenage McCray began scrawling his name on the walls of a correctional facility, an act that became known as tagging. Defacing public property without authorization was and is (4) _____ in America. But McCray continued to tag public spaces across the city, inspiring a generation of young urban artists or writers to use the (5) _____ as their canvas. Their unique art changed the face of the city and gave rise to a new American art form that reflected the (6) _____ nature, diverse identities, and carefree beliefs of America's urban youth during the 70s. This style of art was embraced by many hip-hop artists during the 80s as their aesthetic of choice, which helped to propel graffiti into the (7) _____, changing how advertisers marketed their products and ultimately how art galleries in museums curated their collections.

Today, many Americans view graffiti as an act of vandalism, costing the taxpayer millions of dollars every year to (8) _____ up. Others are drawn to it, flocking to guided tours of the best graffiti spots in America as new generations of artists elevate the art form to new heights, creating pieces that aren't just aesthetically pleasing, but can also raise awareness of important socio-political issues at home and abroad.

Exercise 2

Directions: *Work in groups and answer the following questions.*

(1) What do you think of graffiti? Is it an art form or an act of vandalism?

(2) Why do you think people write graffiti?

Part C Reading for Information

Social Problems in the United States

①Although the United States is a highly developed country, it still has a lot of social problems in its society which need much effort to be improved and finally solved. The following are just among **a myriad of**[1] them.

Poverty as a Social Problem

②Many Americans think of hunger and poverty occurring only in developing countries. While most Americans have encountered someone suffering from hunger and poverty in the United States, few of them may have actually realized it. But the fact is that hunger and poverty in the United States still persist. According to **the US Census Bureau**[2], some 37.25 million people live below the **poverty line**[3] in America in 2020. Evidence shows that millions of families and children live in poverty and experience hunger.

③Many factors contribute to the persistence of hunger and poverty in this nation, including low wages, lack of access to **safety-net programs**[4] including child care and **Food Stamps**[5], inability to take advantage of most tax benefits aimed at middle- and upper-income households, and a lack of opportunity to accumulate savings and other assets.

④Because of its persistence even in times of plenty, hunger and poverty can seem like an **intractable**[6] problem. Yet hunger and poverty do not exist in the United States and around the world because there are not enough resources. The issue is one of priorities. As former Senator Mark Hatfield once said, "We stand by as children starve by the millions because we lack the will to eliminate hunger. Yet we have found the will to develop missiles capable of flying over the **polar cap**[7] and landing within a few hundred feet of their target. This is not innovation. It is a profound distortion of humanity's purpose on earth."

Racism

⑤Loosely defined, racism is the belief that one race is naturally superior to one or more other races. This can lead to behavior, both conscious and subconscious, that **adversely**[8] affects members of the "inferior" race. Judgments such as choosing standard definitions in dictionaries for historically racial terms, where to place waste facilities, and preparing school history books are all affected by the racial attitudes of the decision-makers involved.

⑥Racism is still **alive and well**[9] all over the world. Yet it seems to be on the increase in the United States, after being in decline for decades.

Drug Abuse

⑦Drug abuse in the US has come to be regarded as one of the most challenging social problems facing the nation. The drug issue always excites strong emotions of Americans because drug abuse is perceived as a major threat to American society, particularly to its younger members. Drug abuse is a social problem because it has a wide range of social costs. For example, drugs are closely related with crime and automobile accidents. It has serious effects on individuals physically and mentally, and the economic losses caused by drug abuse are great.

Crime

⑧Crime is one of the most serious problems in the United States. It is generally agreed that violent crime has reached alarming proportions. The murder rate in the United States was five to seven times higher than most industrial nations. The Constitution of the United States **provides**[10] that the right of the people to keep and bear arms shall not be **infringed**[11] upon. It is legal for American citizens to have guns at home. They have access to weapons. The guns that people own may provide a self-protection, but otherwise a killing.

The Abuse of Power

⑨People believe that public organizations in the US sometimes work **in concert**[12] to advance their own interests rather than those of the people. Government in America is widely distrusted for the lack of **answerability**[13]. Americans were convinced that the **Johnson**[14] and **Nixon**[15] administrations were deliberately and systematically lying to the people in the war against Vietnam and in **the Watergate scandal**[16]. The **FBI**[17] and the **CIA**[18] are responsible for some illegal acts. All these acts show the abuse of power by government.

⑩The abuse of power by corporations is reflected in the fact that these corporations are concerned with their own profits than with social responsibility, the quality or price of their products, or the truth of their advertising. They **maintain**[19] professional **lobbyists**[20] in Washington to influence public officials behind the scenes. They argue for legislation to **serve their own ends**[21], influence the appointment of officials, block reforms they consider undesirable, and often seem to have more say in the councils of government than the ordinary voter. Many Americans believe that "big business" has taken the **reins**[22] of government away from Congress and the Administration, and that "government is run by a few big interest groups looking after themselves."

Additional Material

(783 words)

Notes to the Passage

1. a myriad of 大量；许多
2. the US Census Bureau 美国人口普查局
3. poverty line: a level of personal or family income below which one is classified as poor according to governmental standards—called also poverty level 贫困线
4. safety-net programs: plans or systems designed to protect people or prevent serious problems 安全保障计划
5. Food Stamps: a federal program which supplements the food-purchasing ability of low-income households through the distribution of coupons（代金券）which can be used to purchase food for human consumption 发给失业者或贫民的食物券
6. intractable 难处理的
7. polar cap 极地
8. adversely 不利地
9. alive and well 盛行的；依然存在的
10. provide 规定
11. infringe 侵犯；违反
12. in concert 共同地
13. answerability 负责任
14. Johnson: a US politician in the Democratic Party who was the President of the US from 1963 to 1969. He first became president when President Kennedy was killed in 1963, and was elected again in 1964. He then started his plan for a "Great Society" by introducing laws that helped poor people, improved medical care and education, and gave civil rights to all US citizens whatever their race. When the US became more involved in the Vietnam War, however, he became unpopular. 约翰逊 (1908–1973)，美国第17任总统
15. Nixon: a US politician in the Republican Party who was the President of the US from 1969 to 1974. He helped to end the Vietnam War and improved the US's political relationship with China. He is most famous for being involved in Watergate and for officially leaving his position as President before Congress could impeach him (=charge him with a serious crime). Many people thought he was dishonest, and because of this he was sometimes called "Tricky Dicky." 尼克松 (1913–1994)，美国第34任总统
16. the Watergate scandal: also the Watergate ffair, a famous political scandal in the US in the early 1970s that caused President Nixon to leave his job before Congress could charge him with a serious crime. It was discovered that Nixon had agreed to an attempt to obtain information about the Democratic Party's plans for the next election, by secretly going into their offices in the Watergate hotel in Washington D.C. Nixon later tried to prevent this information from being discovered. The Senate asked to hear recordings that Nixon had made of conversations in his office, but when they received them, parts of conversations seemed to have been deliberately removed. These recordings became known as the "Watergate tapes." The Watergate Affair shocked people in the US, and made them less willing to trust their political leaders. Because of these events, other political scandals are often given a name ending in "-gate," for example Irangate. 水门事件

17. FBI (Federal Bureau of Investigation) 美国联邦调查局
18. CIA (Central Intelligence Agency) 美国中央情报局
19. maintain 供养
20. lobbyist 说客
21. serve one's own ends 达到自己的目的
22. rein 统治；支配

Reading Exercise

Directions: *After you read the passage, answer the following questions with the information you get from the passage.*

1. Why do hunger and poverty continue to exist in the US?

_____

2. When may the decision-makers show their racial attitudes?

_____

3. What effects does drug abuse have on drug addicts?

_____

4. What do average Americans think of the US government?

_____

5. Why do corporations argue for legislation?

_____

Part D   Speaking Activities

1. Give Your Ideas

Directions: *Some people are addicted to the Internet. Discuss with each other the possible causes of and solutions to it.*

2. Moment for Sharing

Directions: *Share with each other an American movie you've watched that describes a social problem in the United States.*

3. Armed for Liberty?

Directions: *The Virginia Tech massacre was a school shooting consisting of two separate attacks approximately two hours apart on April 16, 2007, which took place on the campus of Virginia Polytechnic Institute and State University (Virginia Tech) in Blacksburg, Virginia. The perpetrator, Seung-Hui Cho, killed 32 people and wounded many others before committing suicide. This deadly shooting rampage triggers a debate over the justifiability of the public's right to bear arms. Divide your group into two sides, one arguing for the legitimacy of the public's bearing arms, the other against it. The side with more persuasive and convincing arguments wins.*

Chapter 11

Nonverbal Behavior

Part A   Preview

1. The Message Is…

Directions: *Work in pairs and identify what each of the following gestures illustrated might mean.*

2. Guess How I Feel!

Directions: *Work in groups. Use body language to express any of the following emotions and let the rest of the class guess what you are showing them.*

bored, excited, anxious, defensive, relaxed, upset, nervous, fearful, relieved, etc.

Part B   Viewing

How to Read Body Language

Scan and Watch

Vocabulary in the Viewing

deceive 欺骗

rigid 僵硬的

trickery 欺骗，诡计

jerky 抽动的

telltale 泄露秘密的

paranoid 多疑的

twitch 抽搐

fidget 坐立不安

clumsiness 笨拙

averted （尤指目光）移开的

Directions: *Watch the video about how to read body language and answer the following questions.*

1. What is the main idea of the video?
_____

2. How do you know if someone is anxious or nervous?
_____

3. Why did Bush bite the inside of his lip a lot when he was talking?
_____

4. Why do people show signs of over-control?
_____

5. What are some signs of over-control mentioned in the video?
_____

6. How can we learn from the speech that the speaker is lying?
_____

Part C   Reading for Information

Learning Nonverbal Behavior

①When students learn a new language they learn rules of grammar and word meanings, but seldom are the rules of **nonverbal behavior**[1] explained to them. No one explains when to touch or not to touch the individual with whom one is communicating as well as when to smile or not to smile during communication situations. However, successful participation in intercultural communication requires that they recognize and understand culture's influence not only on verbal interaction but on nonverbal interaction as well. Nonverbal behavior, just as does verbal behavior, constitutes messages to which people attach meaning. Nonverbal symbols are derived from such diverse behavior as body movements, postures, facial expressions, gestures, eye movements, physical appearance, the use and organization of space, and the structuralization of time. Such actions vary from culture to culture and are largely unconscious. What might be a sign of greeting in one culture could well be an **obscene**[2] gesture in another. Or what might be a symbol of **affirmation**[3] in one culture could be meaningless or signal **negation**[4] in another.

②The following actions have commonly accepted meanings in the United States:

- Shaking head from left to right—No
- Nodding head up and down—Yes
- Moving extended **index finger**[5] back and forth—A moderate threat or a warning not to do something
- Shrugging the shoulders—"I don't know"
- Rolling the eyes—**Exasperation**[6]
- Looking up in the air and sighing—Strong exasperation
- **Slapping**[7] the knee and smiling—Humor
- Waving the open hand back and forth, palm facing away—Greeting (hello or goodbye)
- Holding the arms out to the side with hands on the waist—"Keep your distance from me" and sometimes anger
- Wrinkling the nose—Disgust; "Something smells"
- Making a circular motion with extended index finger pointed at head—Someone is crazy
- Tapping the toes—Boredom or impatience
- Crossing the fingers—Wishing something will happen; "I'm not telling the truth"
- Winking one eye and smiling—"We are in this together" (**collusion**[8])

③One can learn the meaning of gestures by watching Americans in social situations, but it is more helpful to know some of the common ones in advance. There is some **universality**[9] in some gestures, but it is important to know when such is not the case.

④When Americans greet one another, they often shake hands. There is a nonverbal signal associated with the handshake. One should grasp the other's hand firmly and shake it firmly because to many people in the US a limp handshake indicates a weak person.

Proxemics[10]

⑤Proxemics is the study of how people use personal space or the "bubble" around one that marks the territory between individuals. Different cultures have different views and different rules of personal space. For example, Americans are uncomfortable if people stand too close to them during a conversation. This is in contrast to Middle Easterners and Latin Americans who stand quite close to one another during a conversation. Edward Hall, the anthropologist who has made a life-long study of proxemics, also refers to cultures as contact cultures and non-contact cultures. He has described contact cultures as those societies in which people stand closer together while talking, engage in more direct eye contact, use face-to-face body orientations more often while talking, touch more frequently, and speak in louder voices. He has described the US as a non-contact culture, in which people tend to stand farther apart when conversing, maintain less eye contact, and touch less often. He went on to propose a system of classifying the use of interpersonal space. He said that most Americans exhibited four distance zones, marked particularly by shifts in vocal volume. The intimate zone (contact to **eighteen inches**[11]) usually is reserved for spouses, lovers, and close friends. The personal zone (eighteen inches to **four feet**[12]) includes activities such as chatting, gossiping, playing cards and casual interactions and is the territory of friends and acquaintances. Those whom one does not know well are often kept in the social zone (four feet to twelve feet), the domain of interviews, business transactions, and professional exchanges. The public zone (beyond twelve feet) makes interpersonal communication nearly impossible and often **denotes**[13] status difference between the speaker and listener.

⑥Eye contact is included in proxemics because it regulates interpersonal space. Direct eye contact causes a shortened distance between people, whereas less eye contact increases the distance. Eye contact also communicates meanings about respect and status and often regulates turn-taking. For many US Americans, maintaining eye contact communicates that one is paying attention and showing respect. When they speak with others, most Americans look away from their listeners most of the time, looking at their listeners every 10–15 seconds. When a speaker is finished taking a turn, he or she looks directly at the listener to signal completion. However, some cultural groups within the United States use even less eye contact while they speak. For example, some Native Americans tend to avert eye gaze during conversation. Most Americans become uncomfortable if gazed at too long, thinking that the direct gaze maintained over a long period is signaling unexpected (and often unwanted) interest on the part of the gazer.

The Use of Time

⑦In the United States, the expression "timing is everything" means that the most important factor to success is often not what is done but when something is done. There are many cultural variations regarding how people understand and use time. Edward Hall has also studied the concepts of time cross culturally and has distinguished between **monochromic and polychromic**[14] time orientation. People who have a monochromic concept of time regard it as a commodity. Time can be gained, lost, spent, wasted, or saved, with one event happening at

a time. In general, monochromic cultures value being punctual, completing tasks, and keeping to schedules. The United States is a monochromic culture. For example, most university staff and faculty maintain a monochromic orientation to time. Classes, meetings, and office appointments start when scheduled. Faculty members see one student at a time, hold one meeting at a time, and keep appointments, except in the case of an emergency.

⑧In contrast, in a polychromic society, several events can happen at once. This is true in the Middle East, where US businesspeople often complain that meetings there do not start on time and that people socialize during meetings. International business personnel and students observe that US people

Additional Material

seem too tied to their schedules; they suggest that Americans do not care enough about relationships and often sacrifice time with friends and family in order to complete tasks and keep appointments. On the other hand, Americans are distressed by the manner in which appointments are handled by polychromic people. The importance of time is so woven into the fabric of US culture that Americans are hardly aware of the degree to which it determines and coordinates everything they do. There are many **metaphors**[15] about time, and these should be taken seriously. Time can be saved, spent, wasted, lost, made up, and killed. It can also crawl and run out. Even though the American concept of time must be learned, it is so thoroughly **ingrained**[16] into the US culture that it is treated as though it were the only natural and logical way of organizing life.

Physical Appearance and Dress

⑨Even physical appearance or how a person is dressed may contribute to a stereotype. One individual wrote about the following experience a friend of hers had, based on dress: A close friend I had in high school was very intelligent. He took honors classes and did well in school. He was Hispanic and dressed with **baggy pants**[17] and long shirts. When he went to speak with the counselor upon entering the university, the counselor came to the conclusion that my friend was going to take easy classes rather than honors classes. My friend's appearance obviously caused the counselor to come to a conclusion about who and what type of person my friend was.

⑩The baggy pants and long shirt were a type of nonverbal communication falsely interpreted by the counselor who associated that type of dress with uncaring, poor students. An individual visiting the US or watching US television might mistakenly conclude that this type of dress is appropriate for young people in all situations. Obviously, such is not the case.

⑪In conclusion, the individual visiting the US needs not just a command of the English language but also knowledge of important nonverbal communication strategies. These are harder to **come by**[18], but still possible to find out about in books and by talking with Americans about the subjects mentioned in this chapter.

(1,434 words)

Notes to the Passage

1. nonverbal behavior 非言语行为
2. obscene 猥亵的；淫秽的
3. affirmation 肯定
4. negation 否定，否认
5. index finger 食指
6. exasperation 恼怒，激怒
7. slap 用手掌打
8. collusion 同谋
9. universality 普遍性
10. proxemics 空间关系学（研究人与人在不同社会环境中对空间的需要及人对周围空间感觉的一门学科）
11. eighteen inches 18英寸，约为0.46米

12. four feet 4英尺，约为1.2米
13. denote 表示
14. monochromic and polychromic: In its simplest terms, monochromic time refers to single task management, while polychromic time is analogous to multitasking, carrying forward several activities at the same time. 单一时间和多元时间
15. metaphor 隐喻
16. ingrain 把……深深地印在
17. baggy pants 松垮的裤子
18. come by 得到

Reading Exercise

Directions: *After you read the passage, answer the following questions with the information you get from the passage.*

1. What is critical for successful intercultural communication?

2. What does nonverbal communication include?

3. What does "wrinkling the nose" mean in the United States?

4. What is proxemics?

5. Why does Edward Hall describe the US as a non-contact culture?

6. What are the four distance zones proposed by Edward Hall?

7. What do many Americans mean by maintaining eye contact?

8. Why do most Americans feel uncomfortable if they are gazed at too long?

9. What do you learn from the passage about American way of understanding and using time?

_____

10. Why did the counselor think that the boy would take easy classes rather than honors classes?

_____

Part D Speaking Activities

1. Body Part Idioms

Directions: *Each of the following sentences contains a body part idiom. Complete the sentences by unscrambling the words shown in brackets. Then figure out what these idioms mean based on the context.*

(1) When a girl is really pretty, you might say that she is a sight for sore _____. (e s e y)

(2) "Keep your _____ up" is what you could say to people who you want to cheer up, even though they are in a difficult situation. (i c h n)

(3) When you use all your resources to defend yourself from some attack, you fight tooth and _____. (a n l i)

(4) If you accidentally said something that might have hurt someone else's feelings or embarrassed someone, you might have put your foot in your _____. (t o m u h)

(5) If you want someone to know that you are listening carefully, you can say that you are all _____. (a e r s)

(6) If something is very near to you and you're close to finding it, it is right under your _____. (s o n e)

(7) If someone wants you to be quiet, they may tell you to zip your _____. (p l i s)

(8) If you took too much food than you could eat, maybe your eyes were bigger than your _____. (m s o t a h c)

(9) If someone doesn't dance well or is clumsy, they have two left _____. (f e t e)

(10) If something is bothering you and you need to tell someone, you need to get it off your _____. (e c h t s)

(11) If someone needs help, you can give them a _____. (d a n h)

(12) If you can't quite think of a word but almost get it, that word is on the tip of your _____. (t n o u e g)

(13) The party organizers deserve a pat on the _____ for a job well done. (c k a b)

(14) Trying to find a parking space downtown is really a pain in the _____. (e n k c)

(15) I'm all _____ with repairs and no talent whatever for them. (s b t u m h)

(16) I'll just cross my _____ and wish myself good luck. (g f n i r e s)

2. Test Your Knowledge of Body Language

Directions: *Complete the following quiz to find out how much you know about body language.*

(1) When you approach someone or they approach you, are you aware of the space created between you and the other person?

☐ Yes, I am fully aware of it.

☐ No, I do not notice such things.

(2) Do you feel tense or uneasy if someone is staring at you?

☐ Yes.

☐ No.

(3) When someone you are talking to starts looking away or fidgeting (坐立不安), you _____.

☐ continue to talk

☐ stop talking and/or change the subject

(4) Do you keep comfortable eye contact while conversing with another person?

☐ Yes, I keep good eye contact while talking and occasionally look away.

☐ No, eye contact makes me uncomfortable.

(5) Do you consciously smile when you greet another person?

☐ Yes, I make sure I have a pleasant look on my face when I greet.

☐ No, I am not aware of my facial expressions when greeting someone.

(6) Are you aware of your tone of voice during a conversation?

☐ Yes, my tone of voice is important and I am aware of it.

☐ No, I just talk and don't think about it.

(7) Are you aware of your facial expressions while someone is talking to you?

☐ Yes, I make sure my facial expressions show interest.

☐ No, I just listen without any awareness of my facial expressions.

(8) Do you nervously play with objects or fiddle with things during a conversation?

☐ Yes.

☐ No.

(9) If someone is hesitating a lot during a conversation and not maintaining good eye contact, you _____.

☐ trust what the person is saying

☐ have doubts about what is being said

(10) I find it easy to tell someone's mood just by being with them for a short while.

☐ Yes.

☐ No.

3. Can You Read My Body Language?

Directions: *Work in pairs. Each pair will be given one dialogue.*

Step 1

Each pair works out how they would present the dialogue through mime
and gestures.

Step 2

Each pair works with another pair with a different dialogue, presenting their
mimed versions of the dialogue to each other. Those who are watching need
to observe carefully and think about what the mimes might mean.

Step 3

Each pair tries to write the dialogue for the mime that they just watched.

Step 4

The two pairs that worked together share what they wrote and compare it
with the original dialogue.

4. Cultural Differences in Body Language

Directions: *Work in groups. Each group works on one nonverbal gesture or movement. Observe how
American people use that body language by watching movies and/or observing people around you.
Report to the class on the observations. Then discuss how people from different cultures use that
body language and explore how their differences could make cross-cultural communication difficult.*

*Some possible aspects of nonverbal communication include: eye contact during conversation, eye
contact between strangers passing on a street or hallway, leg crossing, signals used to interrupt
conversation, greeting signals, departure signals, use of hands during conversation, hand-to-
mouth movements, grooming gestures, defensive postures, gestures of children, smiles, distances in
conversation, male/female differences in conversation, positions within a group, territorial markers in
public places.*

Chapter 12

Traffic and Driving

Part A Preview

A Quiz on Traffic Signs in the US

Directions: *Look at the following traffic signs in the US carefully and make the correct choice.*

1.

   A. Stop.

   B. You can walk.

   C. No vehicle can enter.

2.

   A. You should run.

   B. You can walk.

   C. You should wait.

3.

   A. You must stop.

   B. You cannot enter.

   C. Slow down and be ready to stop.

4.

   A. End of speed limit.

   B. No entry.

   C. Clearway (畅行道，禁停公路).

5.

A. Oncoming traffic has priority.

B. Two-way traffic.

C. Oncoming traffic gives way.

6.

A. Buses and taxis turning.

B. One-way system.

C. Mini traffic circle (环形交叉).

7.

A. You cannot make a U-turn.

B. You cannot turn left.

C. You must turn around.

8.

A. Look for cars. Stop and wait if cars are coming.

B. You can walk across the street here.

C. You must stop, even if there are no cars coming.

9.

A. Handicap parking.

B. Pedestrian crossing.

C. Wheelchair convention.

10.

A. Speed limit of 80.

B. 80 miles left to another state.

C. Number of interstate highway.

11.

A. Getting around a roadway that is closed.

B. You may go either way.

C. You must turn right.

12.

A. Deer crossing.

B. Deer dancing.

C. Deer walking.

Part B   Listening

Scan and Listen

Cracking Down on Drunk Driving

Vocabulary in the Listening

campaign 运动

crackdown 镇压，制裁

proven technology 得到证实的技术

alcohol-impaired 受酒精影响的

Mothers Against

Drunk Driving

反醉驾母亲协会

Additional Material

enforcement 实施，强制执行

advocate 提倡者

ignition interlock device 点火联锁装置

sober 清醒的

tactic 策略

Directions: *Listen to the news report on drunk driving and answer the following questions. You may listen again to check your answers.*

1. What is the news report mainly about?
_____

2. What is the device being discussed to stop drunk driving?
_____

3. How many people are killed because of drunk driving every year in Washington D.C.?
_____

4. What are people's general attitudes towards ignition interlock devices?
_____

Part C   Reading for Information

Driving a Car: A "Rite of Passage[1]"

Introduction

①**Anthropologists**[2] have studied the "rite of passage" in nations throughout the world. In other words, there is something in each society that indicates that youths are moving into adulthood. In the United States, more and more individuals agree that getting a driver's license is the real rite of passage, the time that most young people look forward to.

Learning to Drive

②At one time one of the parents (often the father) taught the children of the family to drive. In the 1960's the task was gradually passed along to the school systems. Some of the teachers were given special training as to how to teach students to drive during certain classes known as "drivers education" classes. In these classes the students first study and learn the driving rules of their state, including such things as when lights need to be used, what certain shapes of traffic signs indicate etc. After students feel essentially at ease with the traffic and driving rules, they are tested over their knowledge. Most often these tests are administered by state police officers. The tests are multiple-choice in nature. A person must not miss more than six answers out of thirty. The student is then issued a **learner's permit**[3], indicating that he/she can practice driving with an adult.

③In most driver's education classes the students learn to drive in special automobiles. The driver's education teacher sits in front with the student driver, discusses what should or shouldn't be done etc. Usually two students sit in the rear seat, learning from the mistakes of whoever is driving at one time. The students are also encouraged to practice with their parents in the family car. If there are quiet parking lots or rural roads nearby, one will often see student drivers practicing with a parent until the parent is satisfied that the youngster has learned to handle the automobile safely and carefully. Eventually the student will go back to be tested on his/her driving skills by a state police officer. The officer will require a youngster to drive in busy areas, park, make left turns, etc. If too many errors are made, the student driver will be told to try again at a later time. If the student does well, a driver's license will be issued. That is a very proud moment for a student driver.

④Different states have different laws as to when a person can be issued a driver's license. On farms, children may drive as soon as it is physically possible, as long as they do not drive on public highways. In some rural states it is possible to gain a **provisional license**[4] when one is fourteen years old, but there are various requirements attached to this license. Perhaps the young person will be able to drive only to school, during daylight hours, alone or with another adult. In states with more traffic and **congestion**[5], the age is more often sixteen, or even eighteen.

⑤In many **metropolitan**[6] areas it is common to have commercial driving schools. Trained professional driving teachers are paid a salary and are available to teach persons of **legal driving age**[7], instructing and studying both the knowledge and practice of driving, often with cars which belong to the driving school. These schools prepare the student for taking the state driving test, and their success rate is excellent.

⑥Driver's licenses are in general use for identification. Since drinking laws require that a person be twenty-one years of age in order to be served **alcoholic beverages**[8], the picture of a younger person will be a **profile picture**[9]. That makes it easy to identify the age of the individual. As might be expected, many groups in the US are concerned about drinking and drunk drivers.

Problems in Driving

⑦The US Department of Transportation estimates that alcohol is involved in nearly 75% of driving accidents and even higher percentages of **fatalities**[10] due to alcohol and other drug use by drivers. At the local level, MADD (Mothers Against Drunk Drivers) is one of the most effective organizations working for "anti-drinking education." They work closely with schools and community police and concerned citizens to educate students against driving under the influence of alcohol. At both the high school and college levels, school organizations and even many bars which serve alcohol to young people, urge that any group of students that goes to bars for a party or other reasons, have a person who is the "designated driver." Each person in that group agrees that the designated driver will drink no alcohol, and in many cases the group and/or the bar will provide free non-alcoholic soft drinks to the designated driver. Still, alcohol is a major factor in accidents involving young drivers and other ages as well.

⑧Even when no alcohol use is involved, the current level of traffic makes it important that no type of distraction from safe driving be permitted. Many accidents involve lack of attention by the driver, sleepiness, tiredness, etc. Some individuals may eat or drink while driving, and more recently use of cell phones by the driver has become a major concern.

Traffic Congestion and Driving

⑨Driving has certainly become more demanding as traffic congestion has increased in recent years. About 60 years ago, many states would issue a driver's license without any formal driver's education or testing. Simply by paying a standard fee, one could obtain a driver's license by mail without appearing before an examiner.

⑩Cars go faster now than in the past, depending upon the congestion of the traffic and the road conditions. For example, the speed limits on "**superhighways**[11]," such as interstate highways and **toll roads**[12] may vary from 50 mph in congested areas to as high as 75 mph in more open conditions of Western United States. Speed limits within cities are variable, but usually 35–45 mph in areas of limited access, such as in industrial areas, to 20–25 mph in school zones and residential areas. Fines for speeding may be quite high. For example, driving 10mph over the limit on superhighways may result in a fine from $50 to $75, and speeds beyond this may bring higher fines and even **suspension**[13] of a driving permit for a period of time. Speeding on city streets is often even more costly, especially in school zones or some congested residential areas. **Revocation**[14] of a driver's license is common for drivers with a history of speeding—usually 3 or more **violations**[15] in one year. Even if speed limits are not exceeded, drivers may be fined and may lose a license for having open alcohol containers in the car, careless driving, or driving faster than a safe speed in the case of heavy rain, fog, or snow and ice, for school buses stopped to pick up or leave children at a bus stop, or areas of **limited vision**[16].

Driving and Accident Rates

⑪It is a matter of record that very young and very old drivers have a higher accident rate than middle-aged drivers. For young drivers this is often a result of general inattention to driving and lack of experience and/or judgment. In older drivers, the problem is often related to faulty vision, faulty hearing, or general slower reaction time to traffic problems. Therefore, in most states, the length of the period of a driver's license adjusts from 4 years in drivers up to 70 years of age, to 2 years for those over 70, and finally to one year for very old people who still drive. For all license **renewals**[17], an individual is tested for vision—with or without glasses—hearing, and any evident physical or mental disabilities. Any disability requires a full physical examination and a statement from the individual's **family doctor**[18] that estimates the degree of disability and the risk of driving for the person concerned.

Parking Problems

⑫Another indirect factor in driving and traffic is the availability of parking space for vehicles. In many places, parking garages and **parking lots**[19] are limited. In some cities vehicles are permitted in downtown traffic only **on alternate days**[20], during limited hours in the day, etc. For example, most colleges and universities confront a major problem in **furnishing**[21] parking for all of the students **in attendance**[22]. Many cities will not permit parking on city streets for more than two or three hours, and parking fees are often expensive and limited to faculty and staff, or disabled persons. Many cities also install parking meters which take coins and paper bills or credit cards, often charging between 25 cents to more than a dollar for an hour of parking. This becomes a consideration for any **commuter**[23] who must decide whether it would be more feasible to take mass transportation to his working place or school, factory, etc., or whether it might in fact be better to ride a bicycle, or to join other workers or students in "**car pools**[24]." Some people have resumed walking to work if that is possible, and this means that these cities must provide **sidewalks**[25] and traffic lights to control not only vehicles, but **pedestrian**[26] travel as well.

(1,504 words)

Notes to the Passage

1. rite of passage 标志人生进入一个新阶段的重大事件
2. anthropologist 人类学家
3. learner's permit 见习汽车司机的驾照
4. provisional license 临时驾照
5. congestion 拥堵

6. metropolitan 大都市的
7. legal driving age 合法的开车年龄
8. alcoholic beverage 含酒精的饮料
9. profile picture 头像
10. fatality 死亡者；死亡事故
11. superhighway （美国的）超高速公路

12. toll road 收费道路

13. suspension 暂停

14. revocation 取消；吊销

15. violation 违章

16. limited vision 视觉受限

17. renewal 更新，换新

18. family doctor 家庭医生（指家庭成员经常求诊的一般开业医生，亦称family physician）

19. parking lot 停车处

20. on alternate days（实行）单双号（通行）

21. furnish 供应，提供

22. in attendance 在上学的

23. commuter 通勤者

24. car pool 拼车（一群各有自备汽车的人，安排好在上下班时间每次合乘其中一人之车，并由其开车）

25. sidewalk 人行道

26. pedestrian 行人

Reading Exercise

Directions: *After you read the passage, complete the following sentences with the information you get from the passage.*

1. After students learn the traffic and driving rules, they will take a written test administered by _____.

2. One must get a _____ before he/she can practice driving with an adult.

3. Finally the student will go back to be tested on his/her driving skills by _____.

4. In many metropolitan areas it is common to have commercial driving schools. Trained professional driving teachers are available to teach persons of _____, often with cars which belong to _____.

5. When a group of people go to a party or club, they will have a "_____" who will drink no alcohol, and in many cases the group and/or the bar will provide free non-alcoholic soft drinks to him/her.

6. Revocation of a driver's license is common for drivers with a history of speeding—usually as many as _____ violations in one year.

7. Any disability requires a full physical examination and a statement from the individual's family doctor that estimates the _____ and the _____ for the person concerned.

8. Because of the lack of parking space, commuters may consider taking _____ to their working place or school, factory, etc., _____, or having "_____." Some people have resumed walking to work.

Part D Speaking Activities

1. Interpret Traffic-Related Terms

Directions: *Work in pairs. Interpret the following traffic-related terms into English.*

(1) 参加路考　　_____

(2) 上车训练　　_____

(3) 十字路口　　_____

(4) 人行横道　　_____

(5) 血液中酒精浓度 _____

(6) 换车道　　　_____

(7) 开罚单　　　_____

(8) 系好安全带　_____

(9) 双实黄线　　_____

(10) 白色虚线　　_____

(11) 熄火　　　　_____

(12) 交通违章　　_____

(13) 闯红灯　　　_____

(14) 乱穿马路　　_____

(15) 酒后驾车　　_____

(16) 禁止鸣喇叭　_____

2. You Were Speeding, Sir!

Directions: *Work in groups of three. One acts as a policeman, the second as a husband who is driving, and the third as a wife who is pregnant. A policeman who is patrolling finds a man speeding. He overtakes the man, waves the car to pull off and wants to fine them. Make up a conversation.*

3. Ways to Curb Drunk Driving

Directions: *Read the following data and then discuss the ways to curb drunk driving. You may discuss what each of the following party can do to improve the situation: the government, the mass media, the bar owners, the work unit, the school, the parents, the spouse, the colleagues, the friends and the driver himself/herself.*

Data:

- Alcohol-related motor vehicle crashes kill someone every 30 minutes and nonfatally injure someone every 2 minutes.
- About 18,000 people in the US die each year in alcohol-related motor vehicle crashes, representing 41% of all traffic-related deaths.
- Alcohol impaired driving will affect one in three Americans during their lifetimes.

4. A Survey of Future Car Buyers

Directions: *An automobile company is planning to explore its market and design new models of cars for college graduates. So the company would like to know more about the needs and preferences of the potential buyers so that they can manufacture the right cars. Now you are helping them to conduct a survey. Work in groups of 4 or 5. Design a questionnaire with about 8 questions, which is intended to gather information concerning who will buy what kind of cars, including the maker (厂家), the model (牌子型号), the price, the color, the emission (排量) and when to buy. Also, take gender into consideration. Have at least 30 students as your respondents, including both genders. Finally, write a report with about 150 words and present it orally in the class.*

Chapter 13

Shopping

Part A Preview

1. How Americans Spent Money

Directions: *The following chart indicates how Americans spend every dollar. Take a close look at the figures and discuss their shopping habits.*

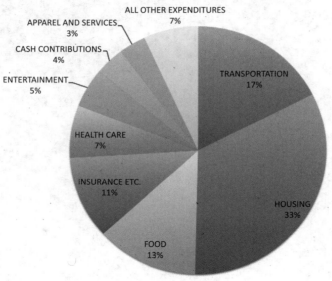

How Americans Spend Money

2. Discussion on Yard Sale

Directions: *Do you have any ideas about good ways to recycle used items? How about having a yard sale? Work in groups and discuss the following questions.*

(1) What is a yard/garage sale?

(2) What are the items in a typical yard sale?

(3) How do you know there is a yard sale somewhere?

3. Similar Sales

Directions: *There are other similar sales of unwanted household goods held in different places in the US. Tick those which are NOT sales for the used items.*

☐ garage sale   ☐ estate sale   ☐ attic sale

☐ moving sale   ☐ spring cleaning sale   ☐ rummage sale

☐ sidewalk sale   ☐ craft sale   ☐ cake sale

☐ warehouse sale   ☐ patio sale   ☐ jumble sale

Part B   Viewing

Online Shopping

Scan and Watch

Vocabulary in the Viewing

collectable 收藏品，珍藏品   diaper 尿片，尿不湿

deodorant 体香剂，除臭剂   e-tailer 网上购物店，电子零售商

lure 诱惑   cut prices to the bone 大减价

equalizer 平衡器   promotional flyer 促销传单

snag 划破处，抽丝处   glitch 小故障，失灵

brick and mortar store 实体店

Directions: *Watch the video about online shopping and choose the best item to complete each of the statements or answer the question.*

1. People like shopping online because _____.

   A. it is easy and convenient

   B. it is unnecessary to leave their house

   C. it can save their time

   D. all of the above

2. People used to buy _____ online.

   A. rare collectables and hard-to-find books

   B. dresses and diapers

   C. perfumes and deodorants

   D. everything

3. E-tailers would try to attract customers by _____.

   A. snatching them away from the mall

   B. offering drastic discounts

   C. distributing promotional flyers

   D. providing them with more options of household goods

4. According to *The Wall Street Journal*, _____ .

   A. customers will always save money when they do shopping online

   B. it is cheaper when they buy all basic items online than they do in stores

   C. the goods bought online can sometimes even be more expensive

   D. customers can be cheated even if they do homework before purchase

5. What is the usual big drawback to shop online according to Donna?

   A. You always have to search for a website.

   B. You always have to match the price with that in the brick and mortar store.

   C. You always have to negotiate with the dealer.

   D. You always have to pay a shipping fee.

Part C Reading for Information

Getting the Most for Your Money

①It might be said that shopping, rather than baseball, is the real national sport of the United States. Apparently that's more than **the Statue of Liberty**[1], **the Empire State Building**[2], or **the Washington Monument**[3], because **the Mall of America**[4], as it is called, asserts that it is the most visited attraction in the United States. More than 1,500 couples have been married in the Mall of America since it opened in 1992.

②Supermarkets in the United States keep getting bigger, and they are always confusing. How can you decide what to buy amid an amazing choice of items? Understanding some general patterns of packaging and pricing can help you evaluate the options available to you. In addition, some helpful guidelines are provided below.

Pricing

③With few exceptions, Americans are accustomed to fixed prices on **merchandise**[5] they buy and sell. The usual exceptions are houses, automobiles, and sometimes major appliances such as refrigerators and washing machines. Americans are not accustomed to **bargaining over prices**[6], and in fact usually feel quite uncomfortable with the idea. Foreign visitors must realize that the price marked on an item does not include the **sales tax**[7] that is added on as part of the payment.

④Americans do not believe, as people from many cultures do, that a commercial **transaction**[8] includes particular attention to the human relationships involved. They look for the item they want, decide whether they can afford the price marked on it, and, if they want to buy it, find a clerk or salespersons to take the money or do the paperwork for a credit-card purchase. People who try to bargain for a low price in a shop or store are likely to be considered either quite odd or startlingly aggressive.

Food Labels

⑤The US grading system for meat has nothing to do with nutrition, only with federal standards of quality for tenderness, juiciness, and flavor. The most common grades of meat are **prime and choice**[9].

⑥Foods are marked using three categories: nutrition information per serving—calories, protein, **carbohydrates**[10], **cholesterol**[11], fat, and **sodium**[12]; percentage of US recommended daily allowances of these items plus vitamins and minerals; and the **ingredients**[13]. It is important to know the size of a serving if you are interested in watching your weight or must eat carefully because of medical conditions such as **diabetes**[14] or heart problems. Many products also have directions for preparation and suggestions for use.

Warnings

⑦Although an increasing effort is being made to protect the buyer, there are still, unfortunately, a number of "**shortcuts**[15]" or hidden factors that one needs to watch out for—sizes and weights, for example. A bottle that looks like a quart (or liter) does not necessarily contain that amount. By law, weight must be printed on all food packages, under "net contents," so one can always check this, but too many of us do not take the time and trouble. Often the print is very small—on purpose!

⑧Such care and study can save you a considerable amount of money on your food bills. The US Department of Agriculture claims that those who watch carefully and who follow the weekly **specials**[16] offered in all supermarkets can save about 6 percent per week. If you have clipped a **discount coupon**[17] from the newspaper and you find the same item on sale in the store, you save even more. And some supermarkets offer "double coupon" savings, meaning you save twice the amount noted on the coupon.

Returning Merchandise

⑨If you have bought something and want to return it, you can do so with most items from nearly all department stores and often, but not always, from smaller shops. However, you must have the **sales slip**[18]. You may return your purchase within 30 days from receipt for a full refund. Clothing returns can be accepted only if the original label/**hangtag**[19] has not been removed. Some stores will take returns without the receipt, but they will refund only the lowest amount the item has sold for. Thus, if it has gone on sale since you bought it, you may get back only a fraction of what you paid. So do not throw away any receipts until you are sure you are satisfied with the item. Sometimes during a sale, the store will post a notice warning customers "All sales are final," which means that you may not return the item for exchange or for your money back.

⑩ If you are returning a gift that has been mailed to you from the store and therefore you have no sales receipt, save the gift slip that accompanies the item and/or take off the delivery label from the front of the package. It has various markings on it that have meaning for the clerk. If you have no label, then ask to exchange for some item of equal worth. It is often easier to do this than to get a cash refund.

Warranties[20]

⑪ When you buy new electrical appliances, radios, TVs, or other major items such as stoves, you will probably be given some papers with them. One of these is likely to be a written warranty. This means that if anything goes wrong, you can have the item repaired free of charge for a certain length of time—for some items as long as three to five years. You should read the warranty carefully. It probably asks you to send in a postcard to establish the date of purchase. If so, be sure to do it as soon as possible. In addition, write the date of purchase on the warranty itself, along with the serial number on the appliance. Keep it somewhere safe so you can find it if you need it.

⑫ The warranty will be of help only if you have saved the papers and complied with the instructions. You may be able to buy an extended service warranty for larger appliances for an additional fee, often up to 25 percent of the purchase price. With the drop in prices of many consumer electronics, you must weigh carefully the cost of such a warranty. With computers, digital cameras, video recorders, and so on, you can be virtually assured that in six months time, you will be able to buy a better model for less money.

Telephone, Catalogue, Internet, and TV Sales

⑬ Telemarketing differs from other sales activities in that it can be carried out by sellers across the country without direct contact with the consumer. However, interstate **telemarketing fraud**[21] has become a problem of such magnitude that the resources of the **Federal Trade Commission**[22] are not sufficient to ensure adequate consumer protection from such fraud.

⑭ One of the largest retail operations in the United States is selling by mail through **catalogues**[23] and through the Internet. Catalogues will arrive in your mail on a regular basis, and you can purchase anything from **gourmet**[24] food to fur coats by mail, phone, or via the Internet. Growth in this sector has occurred for several reasons. People have less time for shopping—especially in two-career families—and retailers can reach a greater number of people. Most important is that shopping by mail is convenient, especially for the elderly or others who cannot move around easily. The disadvantage, of course, is that you cannot try on clothes or examine the products.

⑮The Internet is a popular place for people to buy both new and used goods. You may be amazed at the variety of goods being sold on the Internet. You can buy books, clothing, toys and games, DVDs, and much more. As always, **buyer beware**[25].

⑯There have also been a number of television shows—and even entire 24-hour channels, aimed at the television viewer. These shows feature items at supposedly discounted prices, though you may frequently be able to find comparable prices in local stores. They display a variety of merchandise from clothing, jewelry, clocks, luggage, and toys to small kitchen **gadgets**[26], hardware, and exercise equipment. To order from one of these **TV vendors**[27], you select the item you want, phone in your order, paying by either credit card, **money order**[28], or **check**[29], and wait for your selection to be shipped to you.

⑰A word of caution: many people impulsively order items from these shows that they neither want nor need—and cannot afford. It is all too easy to **get carried away**[30] by TV salespeople urging you to call in immediately to take advantage of this "limited-time" offer. Take care to avoid this situation. Also, quality varies tremendously among these products.

Additional Material

(1,419 words)

Notes to the Passage

1. the Statue of Liberty 自由女神像
2. the Empire State Building 帝国大厦
3. the Washington Monument 华盛顿纪念碑
4. the Mall of America 美国商城（美国最大的购物中心）
5. merchandise 商品
6. bargain over prices 讨价还价
7. sales tax 销售税（在美国大多数州都有销售税，该税不含在商品价格中）
8. transaction 交易
9. prime and choice 极佳级和特选级（美国肉类等级中最好的两级）
10. carbohydrate 碳水化合物
11. cholesterol 胆固醇
12. sodium [化]钠
13. ingredient 成分
14. diabetes 糖尿病
15. shortcut 捷径
16. special 特价商品
17. discount coupon 折扣券
18. sales slip 售货单发票；销售小票
19. hangtag 标签
20. warranty 商品保单
21. telemarketing fraud 电话推销诈骗
22. Federal Trade Commission 联邦贸易委员会（美国政府独立机构，成立于1914年，其主要任务是保护消费者及消除强迫性垄断等反竞争性商业行为）
23. catalogue 商品目录单
24. gourmet 美食

25. buyer beware 买者自负	28. money order 汇票
26. gadget 小器具；小配件	29. check 支票
27. TV vendor 电视购物供应商	30. get carried away 头脑发热

Reading Exercise

Directions: *After you read the passage, answer the following questions with the information you get from the passage.*

1. How are the supermarkets in the United States changing?

_____

2. What kind of price do Americans prefer when they buy and sell?

_____

3. On what items do Americans like to bargain with the dealer?

_____

4. What are the three categories employed to mark food?

_____

5. What should a consumer watch out for to protect himself/herself?

_____

6. Can you return the item you have bought to every store in the US? If you want to return it, what do you have to show to the store?

_____

7. What is the function of a written warranty?

_____

8. Why is shopping by mail popular in the US?

_____

Part D　Speaking Activities

1. Define the Terms

Directions: *Work in pairs. Define the following terms in English.*

(1) mall: _____

(2) bargain: _____

(3) sales tax: _____

(4) sales slip: _____

(5) refund: _____

(6) discount: _____

(7) warranty: _____

(8) coupon: _____

(9) retailer: _____

(10) telephone sales/telemarketing: _____

2. Different Measurements

Directions: *The measurements for clothes and shoes are different from country to country. Please tell the corresponding USA measurements in the table. The first key in each item is provided for your reference.*

Women's clothes	China (cm)		160–165/ 84–86	165–170/ 88–90	167–172/ 92–96	167–172/ 92–96	168–173/ 92–96
	USA	2					
	International	XS	S	M	L	XL	XXL
Men's clothes	China (cm)		165/88–90	170/96–98	175/108–110	180/118–122	185/126–130
	USA		36				
	International		S	M	L	XL	XXL

Women's shoes	China	35	35.5	36	36.5	37.5	38	38.5	39	40	40.5		
	USA	4.5											
Men's shoes	China	39	40	40.5	41	42	42.5	43	44	44.5	45	45.5	46
	USA	6.5											

3. Your Favorite Means of Shopping

Directions: *In the reading passage "Getting the Most for Your Money," we've learned several means of shopping—telephone, catalogue, Internet, TV sales and going to the mall. Among them, which one do you prefer? Give your reasons and share your own experiences. Be sure to give some examples.*

4. How to Have a Yard Sale?

Directions: *There are secrets to having a successful yard sale. The best yard sale requires lots of work, but it's worth it when you count your profits at the end of the day. Read the following sample of a garage sale ad and then draw up a new one of your own. Be sure to make it clear for the potential customers.*

Sample of a Garage Sale Ad

Large Neighborhood Garage Sale

Fri.–Sat. April 22–23

9:00 AM to 2:00 PM

New items will be added as room allows Sat AM

Multi-Families—At 124 thru 126 Lakeside Dr. Go west on Liberty (at the corner of the Mall &

Fagens)—to end of street, turn right on Bluxom to Lakeside Dr.

Lots of parking on gravel—fronts of garages

Chapter 14

Food Culture

Part A   Preview

Names of Vegetables and Fruits

Directions: *Match the following vegetables and fruits with their names in the box.*

Vegetables	____ artichoke	____ asparagus	____ avocado	____ broccoli	____ carrot
	____ celery	____ onion	____ pumpkin	____ snow pea	____ zucchini
Fruits	____ blueberry	____ cantaloupe	____ cherry	____ grapefruit	____ kiwi
	____ lemon	____ mango	____ plum	____ quince	____ raspberry

Part B   Viewing

What Is American Food?

Scan and Watch

Vocabulary in the Viewing

Caesar salad 凯撒色拉   pasta 意大利面

goulash 匈牙利红烩牛肉   hamburger 汉堡包

French fries 炸薯条   pizza 比萨饼

bratwurst 德国式小香肠   cheeseburger 芝士汉堡包

Directions: *Watch the video about American food and decide whether the following statements are true or false. Write a "T" for "True" or an "F" for "False" in the spaces provided.*

☐ 1. Most Americans prefer eating vegetables to eating meat.

☐ 2. All over the United States you can taste international cuisines.

☐ 3. French fries are not a typical American food.

☐ 4. In the US some people enjoy Chinese food but some others enjoy Mexican food.

☐ 5. In a German-style restaurant, you can enjoy music while eating food.

☐ 6. Pasta, pizza and Kung Pao Chicken are all Italian food.

☐ 7. Specials refer to food served to special guests in a restaurant.

☐ 8. Usually, you can order hamburger and cheeseburger in a Japanese restaurant.

☐ 9. Hamburgers are favorite food for Americans.

☐ 10. It is hard for Americans to eat good things from all over the world.

Part C   Reading for Information

Food and Food Customs

①Along with finding a place to stay, finding something to eat is likely to be foremost on your mind when you reach the US. Food is very closely linked to culture, and while most Americans might deny it, there is a dominant style of food that is common there. This passage explores types of restaurants, styles of food, American food habits, and food customs.

Various Types of Restaurants

②Because the United States is home to so many different nationalities, you will be able to find almost any kind of restaurant in the large cities. Listings in the **Yellow Pages**[1] may be by national cuisine or by area of the city or both. Restaurants range widely in price. Many post their menus in the window so you can get an idea of prices before you enter. If not, you may want to ask to see a menu before you are seated, or else just ask about the price range. Appearances from the outside can be **deceptive**[2]—what looks small and **inconspicuous**[3] may turn out to be very expensive, or a nicely decorated place may be quite moderate. It works both ways. You can get a good meal for about five to eight dollars in cafeterias or fast-food chains, but in a medium-priced city restaurant you should expect to pay fifteen dollars and up per person—with wine or drinks extra. Prices in big cities go up fast! Beware of state no-smoking laws in all **establishments serving food**[4]. In most states **patrons**[5] in restaurants are no longer permitted to smoke—and you will be unpleasantly surprised if you light up.

③If you are going to a middle- or upper-level restaurant to dine, telephone ahead for a reservation—the earlier the better. Keep to the time of your reservation or else phone to say you will be late. Good restaurants will not hold reservations for more than a short time. If you are turned away or asked to wait because you have not reserved ahead, don't take it personally. The management has no choice. **Fire laws**[6] are extremely strict about the number of occupants, and unannounced fire inspections are frequent. No restaurant owner dares overcrowd his or her establishment.

④Many mid-level restaurants will not accept reservations and operate **on a first-come, first-served basis**[7]. The only way to find out if a restaurant takes reservations is to call.

Quick and Cheap

⑤Fast-food chains, coffee shops, **delicatessens**[8] (delis), **lunch counters**[9], and **diners**[10] offer quick and inexpensive meals. The food and handling are inspected regularly by government officials, so you can usually feel safe about the food, although you are advised to choose a clean-looking place nonetheless. These places are crowded with people at normal mealtimes, particularly over the lunch hour, but if you eat a little early or a little late, you can usually get a seat without waiting too long. They can be found everywhere, are open long hours, and are useful in keeping your food budget down.

⑥Diners are often found on the **outskirts**[11] of towns. They vary from clean and shiny to rather old and run down. Truck drivers often stop at them because they are likely to have good parking facilities and serve large portions of good food at low prices. Some diners, built from the earliest **prefabricated**[12] buildings, are **remnants**[13] of another era. These have fan clubs with elaborate photographic books devoted to them. You do not generally tip at delis, where you serve yourself, or at fast-food restaurants but you do leave a minimum tip at lunch counters and diners, say 10 to 15 percent.

⑦Fast-food places where a limited menu is precooked and ready for rapid **dispensing**[14] and quick consumption have become very widespread and popular in the United States. Fast-food chains **cater to**[15] millions of people who want quick service and fairly good food in clean, simple surroundings. There is no tipping, though in many cases you are expected to clear your own table and **discard**[16] your trash in the containers provided.

Bars and Pubs

⑧Some American bars are loud, smoky (in some cities, smoking is now prohibited in bars as well as restaurants), and crowded; others are rather dark and meant for quiet conversation. Some bars are now a common meeting place for singles and can be quite lively, with a dance floor and loud music.

⑨Unless you name the brand of alcohol you want, you are likely to get a less expensive "house" brand, which for most people is perfectly acceptable. We don't usually order beer by the pint or half pint, as you would in some countries. Ask for a glass of **draft beer**[17] (usually ten to twelve fluid ounces, or one-third) or a bottle. There are many varieties of American beer, and it is served very cold. Imported beers, **ales**[18], and dark beer, are gaining popularity. Japanese, Chinese, and Mexican beer are often available in good restaurants and bars as well.

⑩US whiskey tends to be sweeter, more **full-bodied**[19], and cheaper than the whiskeys of Scotland or Ireland. Canadian whiskey is light. The main US whiskeys are **bourbon**[20] (made from corn) or a blend of several grains, known as "blended whiskey" and often incorrectly called "**rye**[21]." If you want real rye whiskey, be sure the **bartender**[22] understands. He or she will generally serve the blended type unless you make your desire clear.

⑪If you like your drink at room temperature, be sure to say "No ice, please." Americans like most of their drinks ice cold.

⑫An increasingly popular type of pub is a "**brew house**[23]" or **microbrewery**[24]. These feature a variety of beer and ale styles, some usually made **on the premises**[25]. There are usually very good restaurants on site as well.

Hours of Meals

⑬It is possible to be served a meal at any hour—including all night—in most large cities and many small ones, though you may have to look around a bit.

⑭Some places offer Sunday "brunch" (or you might be invited to a brunch at someone's home). This is a combination of breakfast and lunch, served about 11:30 or noon for late Sunday sleepers. If you are outside a major city, it may be difficult to find a place that is open after 8:30 or 9:30 pm, though lunch counters, diners, and fast-food shops usually stay open late.

⑮In people's homes there is considerable variety as to eating times. The main meal is usually served in the evening, except perhaps on Sundays or holidays, when it may be eaten in the afternoon. In cities people often eat dinner about 7:00 or 7:30 pm. Outside the cities most people dine earlier, at 6:00 or 6:30 pm, or sometimes even earlier. The hour for **cocktail parties**[26] is usually 5:00 or 5:30 pm.

American Food Habits

⑯Many people in this country have **become weight and calorie conscious**[27] and are trying to keep down their weight. This is evident in menus offering low calorie or "weight watchers" meals. Grocery stores now offer a huge array of low-fat, "light," no-fat, or "**low-carb**[28]" foods, from ice cream to soup to snack foods. "Diet" drinks (meaning without sugar but full of artificial **sweeteners**[29]) such as **ginger ale**[30] or cola are also popular.

⑰Waiters in restaurants tend to assume that everyone drinks coffee, especially at breakfast and after dinner, but you do not have to do so! Some people drink coffee (regular or **decaffeinated**[31]) or tea with their meal; others drink wine or just water. When dining out, you can ask for tea, milk, soda, beer, wine, or water if you prefer these to coffee.

⑱The main course in American meals is usually meat, **fowl**[32], or fish, but rarely is more than one of these served at the same meal (except that seafood can be used as an **appetizer**[33]—shrimp cocktail, steamed **clams**[34], **pickled**[35] **herring**[36], or smoked **oysters**[37], for example).

⑲Most Americans eat quickly during the day—that is, breakfast and lunch—unless it is a social, business, or family occasion. There is also another reason for eating fast—others in public eating places are waiting for you to finish so they too can be served and get back to work on time. The evening meal, however, is usually leisurely and a family time—unless, of course, there are children involved in sports or other late-afternoon activities.

Additional Material

⑳There is a real difference in leisure and timing here between a meal that is "social," meaning shared and enjoyed, and one that is "just a meal."

(1,413 words)

Notes to the Passage

1. Yellow Pages 电话黄页
2. deceptive 迷惑人的，靠不住的
3. inconspicuous 不显眼的
4. establishments serving food 出售食物的机构（此处指餐厅和饭店）
5. patron 顾客，尤指老主顾
6. fire law 消防法
7. on a first-come, first-served basis 先来先享受服务的原则
8. delicatessen 熟食店
9. lunch counter 便餐馆；速食餐厅的长柜台
10. diner 餐车式饭馆

11. outskirt 郊区

12. prefabricated（尤指建筑）预制的

13. remnant 剩余的人或物

14. dispense 分发；上菜

15. cater to 供应伙食；满足；迎合

16. discard 丢弃，抛弃

17. draft beer 生啤酒

18. ale （淡色）浓啤酒，麦芽酒

19. full-bodied 醇厚的，浓郁的

20. bourbon 波旁威士忌

21. rye 黑麦威士忌

22. bartender 酒吧招待

23. brew house 酿酒屋

24. microbrewery 微型酿酒厂

25. on the premises 店内

26. cocktail party 鸡尾酒会

27. become weight and calorie conscious 关注自己的体重和卡路里摄入量

28. low-carb (=low-carbohydrate) 低碳水化合物

29. sweetener 甜味剂

30. ginger ale 姜汁汽水

31. decaffeinated 脱咖啡因的

32. fowl 家禽

33. appetizer 开胃食品

34. clam 蛤，蛤蜊

35. pickled 腌制的

36. herring 鲱鱼

37. oyster 牡蛎

Reading Exercise

Directions: *After you read the passage, complete the following sentences with the information you get from the passage.*

1. Many American restaurants post their _____ in the window so you can get an idea of prices before you enter.

2. If you are going to a middle- or upper-level restaurant to dine, telephone ahead for a _____—the earlier the better. However, many mid-level restaurants will not accept _____ and operate on _____ basis.

3. Fast-food chains, coffee shops, delis, lunch counters, and diners offer _____ and _____ meals.

4. Truck drivers often stop at small restaurants on the outskirts of towns because they are likely to have good _____ and serve large portions of good food _____.

5. In a bar or a pub, the _____ will generally serve the blended type unless you make your desire clear.

6. If you like your drink at room temperature, be sure to say "_____." Americans like most of their drinks _____.

7. _____ is a combination of breakfast and lunch, served about 11:30 or noon for late Sunday sleepers.

8. Waiters or waitresses in restaurants tend to assume that everyone drinks _____, especially at breakfast and after dinner, but you do not have to do so! When dining out, you can ask for _____, or water if you prefer these to _____.

9. The main course in American meals is usually _____, but rarely is more than one of these served at the same meal.

10. Most Americans eat _____ during the day—that is, breakfast and lunch—unless it is a _____ occasion.

Part D   Speaking Activities

1. Discussion of the Chain Fast-Food Restaurants

Directions: *Work in groups and introduce the most popular chain fast-food restaurants in the United States. Each group is assigned one restaurant. Report to the whole class its history, scale, and special food it sells.*

2. Taboos at the Table

Directions: *Work in groups and list as many taboos at the table in the US as possible.*

3. Role Play

Directions: *Role play a dialogue in pairs. Suppose you are in an American restaurant. A acts as a waiter or waitress while B acts as a diner. A is greeting B and B is asking for a table for four in a non-smoking section. A is showing B a menu, and B is trying to order. At the end of the meal, B offers A a tip because of his/her good service.*

Chapter 15   Animals

Part A   Preview

Interesting Facts about Animals

Directions: *Read the following statements about animals. Half of them are true while half are false. Work in pairs and tick (√) the ones that you think are most likely to be true.*

Statements about Animals	
1. Chickens can swallow while they are upside down.	
2. Zebras can't see the color orange.	
3. Dolphins sleep with two eyes open.	
4. The right leg of a chicken is more tender than the left one.	
5. Rhinos have the highest blood pressure of any animal.	
6. Bulls are color blind.	
7. A goldfish a memory span of 10 seconds.	
8. US Secret Service sniffer dogs are put up in five-star hotels during overseas presidential visits.	
9. A jellyfish is 70% water.	
10. A lion's roar can be heard from five miles away.	
11. No two zebras have stripes that are exactly alike.	
12. Fish is the only animal that can't jump.	
13. Mosquitoes have 2 teeth.	
14. Cats can't taste sweets.	
15. A dolphin's hearing is so acute that it can pick up an underwater sound from fifteen miles away.	
16. Camels have five eyelids to protect themselves from blowing sand.	

Part B   Viewing

Groundhog Day

Scan and Watch

Vocabulary in the Viewing

Groundhog Day 土拨鼠日

hibernation 冬眠

dub 把……称为

festivity 庆祝活动

quell 减轻

onset 开始

immigrant 移民

outlet 地方广播电台（或电视台）

tuxedo 晚礼服

déjà vu 似曾相识

Directions: *watch the video about Groundhog Day and answer the following questions.*

1. On which day is Groundhog Day celebrated each year?
_____

2. How does a groundhog predict the incoming weather?
_____

3. Who first trusted an animal to predict the weather?
_____

4. When and where did the first Groundhog Day celebration occur?
_____

5. What is the name of the group of individuals who take care of the groundhog named Phil?
_____

6. To what extent have Phil's predictions been accurate, according to studies?
_____

7. What new meaning has "Groundhog Day" taken after the 1993 comedy *Groundhog Day*?
_____

8. Where is Groundhog Day mostly observed?
_____

Part C   Reading for Information

The Importance of Pets

Introduction

①In 2007 an extremely wealthy woman in California left twelve million dollars to her dog in her will. She wanted to be certain that her precious pet would always be cared for. While this is an extremely rare case, it is illustrative of the importance of pets in the United States. Not only are they important to those who own them, but according to the 2021–2022 **National Pet Owners Survey**[1], conducted by the American Pet Products Association, pet ownership is at an all-time high in the United States, with 90.5 million households (70 percent of all US households) owning at least one pet. The first survey, conducted in 1988, reported 51 million pet-owning homes. Consequently, it is easy to conclude that pet ownership is increasing in popularity all of the time.

②When thinking of households with pets, one usually first thinks of dogs and cats; however, there are many other types of pets kept by individuals. The 2013–2014 National Pet Owners Survey also had statistics about ownership of the different kinds of pets. Here are the numbers of the US households that own a pet, by type of animal.

- 69 million dogs
- 45.3 million cats
- 6.2 million small animals such as rabbits, **guinea pigs**[2], **hamsters**[3], and white mice
- 2.9 million saltwater fish
- 5.7 million **reptiles**[4]
- 3.5 million horses

Therapeutic[5] Value

③Pets can help humans in various ways. **Seeing Eye dogs**[6] for the blind are universally known, but few people realize that there are also "Hearing Ear" dogs for the deaf. Dogs can also be trained to retrieve and carry things for people confined to wheelchair and bed. Although not as common, small monkeys are sometimes also trained to help these people. Learning to ride a horse can help to put a handicapped child on a more equal basis with normal children. Therapists have noted an improvement in muscle tone, self-confidence and spirits of handicapped children as a result of horseback riding.

④The value of pets to people with various physical **ailments**[7] is just beginning to be explored. In a pioneering study, researchers at the University of Pennsylvania's Center for the Interaction of Animals and Society showed that among 92 victims of heart disease, significantly more pet owners survived for at least one year than did those without pets. Twenty-eight percent of those without a pet died in a year, whereas only 6 percent of those with pets had died. Another study coming from the University of Pennsylvania reported that watching fish in a tank lowers blood pressure, promotes relaxation and counters the adverse psychological effects of stress. Additionally it has been suggested that the importance of touching animals is a source of comfort that might not come from people. It has already been demonstrated that stroking a cat or a dog that a person is fond of will lower that person's blood pressure.

⑤Many accounts have been written of the therapeutic value of animals. More and more care facilities for the elderly allow, in fact encourage, the presence of gentle dogs and cats as visitors. These animals often help a patient to regain interest in life as he/she looks forward to a visit from a four-legged "friend." One mental health specialist who went to New York City several months after the World Trade Center attack to provide disaster mental health services soon realized the value of pets. She worked with people who had lost almost everything and had only their pets left. Their homes, jobs, colleagues, sometimes family members, and often hope were gone. They **hung on to**[8] their pets for support.

⑥One woman's recovery came when she began to care for several cats that were displaced by the **aftermath**[9] of the fall of the towers. She had been the kind of person who took care of her neighbors, but had been disabled in the collapse of the towers. She was depressed about the 9/11 events and about having to stay in her house. Then she noticed three very hungry and frightened cats. She fed them and the cats bonded with her and gave renewed purpose to her life.

Love Your Pets

⑦There are a number of things that help to guarantee the welfare of pets. For example, there are many pet clinics staffed with well-trained **veterinarians**[10]. These veterinarians must be certified as competent by the state in which they reside and work. A pet owner can purchase pet insurance, so if it becomes needful for the pet to have some special medical services, they

will be paid for through the insurance policy. Also there are a number of ways in which pets can be cared for if their owners must leave town. This includes **kennels**[11], where the animals will be fed, watered and exercised. Many times these kennels are also run by veterinarians. Additionally, there are **pet sitters**[12], who will come to the home daily to care for the pet. These services are not cheap, but most pet owners are quite willing to pay for the guarantee that their pets will be cared for well.

⑧Magazine editors, knowing how people love their pets, often publish articles that give advice on pet care. One article on holiday pet safety in a very popular magazine widely read by women gave advice about common items at Christmas time that could be dangerous to a pet. For example, many homes have a Christmas tree that is placed in a container of water. It is tempting for a dog or cat to drink some of this water and the article warned that tree fertilizers could contaminate the water, breed bacteria and cause the animal to become ill. The article also stressed that there is often a lot of chocolate candy around then and it can be very dangerous to dogs in particular, who love to eat it if given the opportunity. However, it can cause kidney failure in a dog so is extremely dangerous.

⑨Many individuals in the US believe that animals have rights. According to the animal rights philosophy, non-human animals have the basic rights of life, liberty and freedom from suffering as humans do. The animal rights movement strives to raise the status of animals beyond that of just property or commodities for human use. Those who believe in animal rights believe that animals have their own inherent right to exist and deserve not to be killed, kept in **captivity**[13] or tortured by humans. Although individuals within the animal rights movement may hold varied opinions about different animal issues, the movement as a whole opposes the use of animals for food, clothing, entertainment, research and other human gain.

⑩In fact, there are a number of rather powerful organizations devoted to the rights and concerns of animals, including the **American Society for the Prevention of Cruelty to Animals**[14] and the **Humane Society of the United States**[15]. Thousands of people contribute annually to these societies in hopes of guaranteeing the welfare of animals. Also many cities and towns maintain animal **rescue shelters**[16], where animals that have been lost or can no longer be cared for by their owners can be cared for until adopted by someone else. These rescue shelters often advertise the available pets on television or in newspapers.

⑪Many other nationalities would say that Americans pay too much attention and spend too much money on their pets, but most US pet owners would feel quite justified in arguing that their pets are worth every penny spent on them and could give many reasons for justifying what they say.

(1,253 words)

Notes to the Passage

1. National Pet Owners Survey: published every year by the American Pet Products Association. It is the most comprehensive consumer research providing insight on demographics, buying habits, and other traits of US owners of dogs, cats, fish, birds, equine, reptiles, and small animals. 全国宠物主人调查

2. guinea pig 豚鼠

3. hamster 仓鼠

4. reptile 爬行动物

5. therapeutic 治疗的

6. Seeing Eye dog 导盲犬

7. ailment 病痛

8. hang on to 依赖

9. aftermath 后果；结果

10. veterinarian 兽医

11. kennel 狗窝；（驯养或寄养狗的）养狗场

12. pet sitter （替别人）照看宠物的人，宠物保姆

13. captivity 囚禁

14. American Society for the Prevention of Cruelty to Animals: The American Society for the Prevention of Cruelty to Animals (ASPCA) is the nation's first humane organization. The ASPCA's mission is to promote humane principles, prevent cruelty and alleviate pain, fear and suffering in animals. 美国防止虐待动物协会

15. Humane Society of the United States: The Humane Society of the United States (HSUS) is the nation's largest animal protection organization. The HSUS is a mainstream voice for animals, with active programs in companion animals, disaster preparedness and response, wildlife and habitat protection, marine mammals, animals in research, and farm animal welfare. 美国人道主义协会

16. rescue shelter 救助站

Reading Exercise

Directions: *After you read the passage, answer the following questions or complete the sentences with the information you get from the passage.*

1. The story of the Californian woman illustrates _____.

2. The 2021–2022 National Pet Owners Survey shows that pet ownership is _____ _____.

3. What animal is the most popular pet among Americans?

_____.

4. Horseback riding helps handicapped children by improving _____.

5. It was observed by one mental health specialist that those who survived from the 9/11 attack depended on their pets for _____.

6. The woman who had been disabled in the 9/11 attack found _____ in caring for cats.

7. Pet clinics, pet insurance and pet sitters are examples of different ways to _____.

8. Chocolate candy can be dangerous to dogs because _____.

9. Animal rights activists are opposed to the use of animals for _____.

10. Where do stray animals stay before they are adopted?

_____.

Part D   Speaking Activities

1. Eight Things You Can Do to Help Animals

Directions: *Work in groups to make a list of eight things you can do to incorporate animal rights into your everyday living. Remember to explain the list with some details.*

2. A World Without Animals

Directions: *Work in groups of four or five. Discuss what the world might be without animals. Then prepare a short play based on the discussion. You may set the play at some time after the disappearance of animals from the earth. Try to reveal the impact of animals on different people, such as vegetarians, doctors, children, senior citizens, farmers, professors, fashion designers, scientists and so on.*

Additional Material

3. Man and Animals

Directions: *Choose one of the following topics that you feel particularly strongly about and give a speech on the issues involved. Remember to support your opinions with examples, statistics, pictures, and so on.*

Topics: factory farming, vegetarianism/veganism, animal testing, pros and cons of zoos, animal law and policy, leading animal rights organizations

4. Animal Welfare Day

Directions: *You are going to set up an Animal Welfare Day to inform students and faculty of some of the issues animals face in the world today. Discuss in groups what activities you might include on that day.*

5. Animals in the American Culture

Directions: *Work in groups to introduce an animal that is closely related to the American culture. Your introduction should focus on the cultural significance of the animal. The following animals are for your reference:*

bald eagle, elephant, donkey, turkey, bison...

Chapter 16

Behavior in Public Places

Part A　Preview

1. Six Most Unpleasant Behaviors on Campus

Directions: *Work in groups to make a list of six most unpleasant behaviors on campus.*

2. What Is Public Behavior?

Directions: *Read the following quote and discuss with your partner your understanding of it.*

"Public behavior is merely private character writ large."

—Stephen Covey

Part B　Listening

Etiquette

Scan and Listen

Vocabulary in the Listening

etiquette 礼节，礼仪	pervasive 普遍的
rule of thumb 经验法则	cubicle 小隔间
resemble 类似于	dash off 迅速写（或画）

Directions: *If you asked Americans a few decades ago for examples of bad manners, they might have mentioned refined points of etiquette, like using the wrong fork for their dinner salad. So what do Americans today consider as rude behavior? Caroline Tiger, the author of How to Behave: A Guide to Modern Manners for the Socially Challenged, and an editor and reporter for the Philadelphia Inquirer, addresses this question in an*

interview. Listen to the interview and complete the following sentences. You may listen again to check your answers.

1. Caroline Tiger believes that people are too _____ to remember about their manners.
2. In the 21st century, good manners are defined as _____.
3. Before people talk on the phone, first they have to _____.
4. Those who are talking on cell phones in public places should _____.
5. Cubic walls are different from actual walls in that _____.
6. In order to be a good cubicle neighbor, people should keep their voice down and keep personal calls _____.
7. When people write e-mails, they should make sure they send them to _____.
8. Caroline Tiger finds it especially irritating that people walking with huge golf umbrellas take up _____ on the sidewalk.

Part C Reading for Information

Behavior in Public Places

Introduction

①With few exceptions we live in groups, and humans are, by nature, **gregarious**[1] persons, carrying out many of their activities in public places. Each society has its expectations for acceptable behavior in public places. While these vary somewhat in different parts of the United States, most of these have common behavioral threads which bind our society together. Americans like to boast of their freedom of expression, but there is a common phrase that states, "Freedom to act or behave ends at the point that it interferes with the freedom of another person." To avoid unpleasant situations there are both civil laws and common sense expectations of behavior in public.

Physical Contact

②Public places are often crowded at certain times of the day, or on special occasions, so one should avoid excessive physical contact with others. **Bumping into**[2] another person may not only inconvenience others, but may cause physical pain or injury to the persons involved. It is important that one be aware of other people in order to avoid bumping into them. Riding a bike, carrying a suitcase, running, or even hurriedly walking in crowded conditions is inconsiderate of others, and unsafe as well. Most cities have laws against careless movement on public streets, sidewalks, and other public places.

③Purposely touching another person's body in public is also unacceptable behavior, especially if it is related to sexual intimidation or exploitation. Even patting another person on the shoulder, gently pushing them, leaning against them, or touching their face or hair is considered bad manners, and unacceptable in public places such as on sidewalks, streets, or on public transportation. Offenders will often be asked to stop the behavior, or sometimes be reported to the police or other officials.

Noise and Noise Pollution

④Loud noises in public places are considered rude and unacceptable in the US One should avoid **honking a car horn**[3], shouting loudly at another person, or making it difficult for other persons to hear instructions, quiet conversations, etc. Even in less crowded conditions, loud noises can be troublesome and are not permitted—by law—near churches, school yards, some parks, etc.

⑤Even emergency vehicles are asked to reduce noise in some public areas, and most cities attempt to control noise pollution at levels that might disrupt other people. Generally, noise levels above 90 **decibels**[4] are not acceptable in public places, so vehicles with loud **exhaust/ muffler noises**[5], loud radios, tape or disk players are prohibited from making loud noises. Offenders may be punished if they fail to comply with these **ordinances**[6].

⑥Some types of behavior that is acceptable in sports stadiums, race tracks, etc. are not appropriate for other public places.

Toilets

⑦The most important phrase you should learn is "Where can I find a toilet?" If you need to visit the toilet, nearly any word will do. All of the following words will work: men's room (women's room), restroom, lavatory, toilet, and bathroom.

⑧There are few public toilets on the streets in the US. Public toilets can usually be found in hotels, bars, restaurants, museums, department stores, gas stations, airports, train stations, and bus stations. Some businesses may reserve their restrooms for the use of their patrons.

⑨In many airports, toilets and **urinals**[7] do not have a **flush**[8] handle, but instead flush automatically when an **infrared sensor**[9] determines that you have left. If you don't see anything that looks like a flush handle, step away from the toilet and see if it flushes after a few seconds.

⑩Restrooms usually supply toilet paper, liquid soap, and disposable paper towels. Often there is also a baby changing station where one can change **diapers**[10] for babies.

Form of Address

⑪American names are written and spoken with the given name first and the family name last. So

John Smith's family name is Smith, not John.

(12) In a formal setting, address men as "Mister" (abbreviated as "Mr."), married women as "Misses" (abbreviated as "Mrs."), and unmarried women as "Miss" (abbreviated as "Ms."). These days many women prefer to be addressed using the abbreviations "Ms." or "M.," pronounced "miz." If the person has an M.D. or Ph.D., they will often be addressed as "Doctor" (abbreviated as "Dr.").

(13) In an informal situation, Americans will introduce each other by first name, without titles, and occasionally by just the last name. If you are introduced to somebody by first name, you can address him or her by first name the next time you meet. The only exception would be for someone who holds an important position, such as the university president or **provost**[11]. Unless they tell you otherwise, faculty should be addressed using their title and last name (e.g., "Professor Smith").

(14) When in doubt, use the formal manner of address, since it is better to **err**[12] on the side of formality. It is also appropriate to ask how they prefer to be addressed.

Etiquette

(15) Rules of etiquette are taught and enforced for individuals and small groups and for use in public places. Beginning with "Please" and "Thank you" expressions, both parents and teachers instruct in manners, positive behavior and politeness as well as respect for other persons. Inappropriate etiquette or misbehavior is not tolerated and good behavior is rewarded. Many colleges and universities include instruction in "table manners" and other etiquette expected of **cultured**[13] individuals. Some residence houses, **fraternities**[14], **sororities**[15] and dormitory cafeterias require some "formal dining meals" where students and student servers are expected to demonstrate proper etiquette in eating and serving as well as appropriate table conversation.

(16) There is also etiquette to be considered on **escalators and moving sidewalks**[16]. It's "Stand right—walk left." If you are going to remain **stationary**[17] while riding the escalator or the moving sidewalk, stand single file on the right side, allowing people who are walking to pass you by on the left side. It's just like

Additional Material

driving—slow moving (or non-moving) people stay to the right and out of the way of faster moving traffic.

Display of Affection

(17) While display of affection between two persons is generally understood, it is usually not acceptable in public if **carried too far**[18]. Friends may kiss or hug one another when meeting, especially at airports, bus terminals, etc., but prolonged physical contact is normally frowned upon, and **petting**[19], **fawning**[20] or display of excessive emotions or speech with one another in public is considered unacceptable behavior. It may be perfectly acceptable in private and intimate meetings between close friends, lovers, or close family members, but not in public.

⑱**Courtship**[21] behavior is usually unexpected and unacceptable in public, and it is apparent that most people prefer to see it restricted to more private settings.

Personal Hygiene[22]

⑲From commercials and elsewhere, Americans are taught that the odors a human body naturally produces—those of **perspiration**[23], oily hair, and breath—are unpleasant or even offensive. A person who follows what Americans consider to be good hygiene practices seeks to control such odors.

⑳The popular conception in American culture is that people should bathe or shower at least once daily, using soap (some varieties of which supposedly contain "deodorant"). People should also brush their teeth with **toothpaste**[24] at least twice a day, if not more frequently, and should use an **underarm**[25] deodorant to control perspiration odor. They should also wash their hair as often as necessary to keep it from becoming oily.

㉑American drugstores and supermarkets have entire aisles filled with personal hygiene products designed to meet these needs. There are countless deodorants made especially for men and for women. Toothpaste comes in many varieties, not only to combat **cavities**[26] but also to whiten teeth and freshen breath. Breath sprays, mints, mouthwashes, and chewing gums are available to supplement the freshening effects of toothpaste. In fact, an entire industry has grown up around personal care products.

㉒In addition, people often use perfume, **cologne**[27], "body splash," and other scented products to give themselves an odor that others will presumably find pleasant. Although women used to be the target market for scented bathing and after-bath products, more and more men now use them also. The ideal person does not use too much of a scented product, however. Too much means that the scent is **discernible**[28] more than three or four feet away from the person's body.

㉓Many Americans regard the sight of hair on or under a woman's arms or on her legs as masculine, unattractive, or **unhygienic**[29]; most American women shave their legs and under their arms. A small number of women choose not to shave at all.

㉔According to the general American conception, clothing, like bodies, should not emit unpleasant **aromas**[30]. Americans generally believe that clothing that takes on the smell of the wearer's perspiration should be washed before it is worn again. For many, this means washing their clothes after each wearing, particularly during warm summer months.

Conclusions

㉕In American society, as in most other traditions, a visitor may be advised, "When in Rome, do as the Romans do." By watching the behavior of most of the people in public, it is not difficult to recognize what is acceptable behavior and what isn't.

㉖By watching the etiquette at a dinner table, it is helpful to observe the host or hostess as they select the appropriate **utensils**[31] for eating, the levels of conversation and voice, etc. By watching the behavior as lines are formed for service in a restaurant, bus and train transportation, hailing a taxi, etc., one can see and appreciate regional differences which exist and which reflect the diversity and the common practices of behavior in public.

(1,580 words)

Notes to the Passage

1. gregarious （爱）群居的
2. bump into 撞到，撞上
3. honk a car horn 鸣汽车喇叭
4. decibel 分贝（表示功率比和声音强度的单位）
5. exhaust/muffler noise 排气管/消声器噪音
6. ordinance 法令；条令
7. urinal 小便处，小便池
8. flush 冲洗
9. infrared sensor 红外线感应器
10. diaper 尿布
11. provost （美国某些大学的）教务长
12. err 犯错误
13. cultured 有教养的，有修养的
14. fraternity 兄弟会
15. sorority 姐妹会
16. escalators and moving sidewalks 自动扶梯和自动人行道

17. stationary 不动的
18. carry sth. too far 把某事做得过分
19. pet 抚弄
20. fawn 奉承，讨好
21. courtship 求爱
22. hygiene 卫生
23. perspiration 汗；出汗
24. toothpaste 牙膏
25. underarm 腋下的
26. cavity （牙的）蛀洞
27. cologne 古龙香水
28. discernible 辨别得出的
29. unhygienic 不卫生的
30. aroma 气味；香味
31. utensil 器皿

Reading Exercise

Directions: *Read the following statements and decide whether they are true or false according to the passage you have read. Put a "T" for "True" or an "F" for "False" in the spaces provided. If the statement is false, explain why.*

☐ 1. Americans generally dislike physical contact with others.

☐ 2. Purposely touching another person's body in public is often related to sexual intimidation.

☐ 3. In the US, the noise exposure limit in public places is set at 90 decibels.

☐ 4. People do not have to bring their own toilet paper when they go to a public toilet.

☐ 5. The purpose of "formal dining meals" at fraternity and sorority houses is to reinforce the emotional bond between students.

☐ 6. On escalators and moving sidewalks, stand to the right so that others may pass by you on the left.

☐ 7. Display of affection between two persons is not acceptable in public places.

☐ 8. Americans generally believe that people should bathe or shower twice a day.

☐ 9. Many companies have started to target their scented bathing and after-bath products at both men and women.

☐ 10. Most American women choose not to shave their legs and under their arms.

Part D   Speaking Activities

1. Translation of Useful Expressions

Directions: *Translate the following expressions related to behavior in public places and personal hygiene.*

(1) 个人卫生 _____

(2) 冲澡 _____

(3) 油腻的头发 _____

(4) 汗味 _____

(5) 先到先得 _____

(6) 挡住视线 _____

(7) 右侧通行 _____

(8) 体味 _____

(9) 化妆 _____

(10) 散发不良气味 _____

(11) 入乡随俗 _____

(12)（排队时）插队 _____

(13) 禁烟区，无烟区 _____

(14) 身体接触 _____

(15) 一次性纸巾 _____

(16) 洗衣服 _____

2. To Be Polite

Directions: *Work in pairs to decide whether the following statements are true or false in the United States. Write a "T" for "True" or an "F" for "False" in the spaces provided. If you think a statement is false, try to work out what should be said or done in the particular situation.*

☐ (1) It is considered impolite if you do not say "I'm sorry" when you bump into somebody accidentally in a corridor, or a crowded place.

☐ (2) In the United States when people are first introduced, they usually shake hands.

☐ (3) When you answer the telephone in the United States, you should always start by giving your name.

☐ (4) When you go into a shop in the United States, you should always address the shopkeeper as "Sir" or "Madam."

☐ (5) If you want to attract the attention of someone you do not know, you should use "Sir" with a rising intonation.

☐ (6) When you want to attract a waiter in a restaurant in the United States, you would loudly snap your fingers and say "waiter" in a loud voice.

☐ (7) When you enter a railway compartment or a room which is full of strangers in the United States, you should greet each of the people present. You will be considered impolite if you do not.

☐ (8) When you greet someone in the United States, it shows your concern if you ask after their health.

☐ (9) When you are on the phone, it is normal to signal that you are about to end a conversation by using expressions such as "Look, I've got to go," or "I'll let you get back to what you're doing."

☐ (10) In the United States it is polite to ask a person's age or salary as a way of getting to know them.

3. Role Play

Directions: *Work in pairs. Role play the dialogue according to the description on the role card each of you receives from the teacher.*

Situation 1: A and B are the only passengers in a train compartment.

Role A

You love speaking English. You also love to talk and to find out everything about other people, even if this means asking very personal questions. What is wrong with personal questions, anyway? Try to find out as much as possible about the other passenger, who must be an American (you have seen the name tag on the suitcase).

Role B

You are an American. You dislike talking about yourself but you hate being rude, so you can never tell anybody to mind their own business. Say as little about yourself as possible. Be evasive. Try to divert the other person's attention. (You have reserved your seat, so you cannot leave the compartment!)

Situation 2: The conversation takes place in a restaurant.

Role A

Last week you gave up smoking. You are sitting in a restaurant waiting to be served. The man at the next table is smoking and all the smoke is coming in your direction. He looks rich, arrogant and foreign. You are not in a mood for a quarrel but smoke has really been getting on your nerves lately. You decide to begin a seemingly casual conversation and then, gradually, get round to asking the man to do something about the cigarette: put it out, hold it in the other hand… anything! You begin.

Role B

You are a chain-smoker. You are smoking now. You are sitting in a restaurant waiting to be served. The woman at the next table looks very friendly. You feel rather bored and wouldn't mind a chat, especially since you are talkative. You have a tendency to interrupt people before they finish what they want to say. You like telling them your life story.

Situation 3: A and B are roommates.

Role A

B is your roommate. He has an offensive body odor since he doesn't take a shower even after he works out at the gym. He changes his clothes only once a week. And he smells like a garlic factory! But you don't want to sound rude.

Role B

A is your roommate. He often uses cologne. You think A cares too much about how he looks and smells. And you believe a more natural smell is better than an artificial one. But you consider the subjects of body odor too embarrassing for men to discuss.

4. A Survey on Mobile Phone Use in Public Places

Directions: *Work in groups and conduct a survey on the use of mobile phones in public places, such as cinemas, classrooms, restaurants, libraries, banks and so on. Try to explore the issue from many different perspectives, such as mobile phone etiquette, sending a text message vs. making a voice call, different people's attitude toward mobile phone use in public, etc. You may present the result of your survey in any form that you find appropriate, such as an interview, an oral report, or a short play.*